The Campaign of Magenta and Solferino, 1859

D1452657

The Campaign of Magenta and Solferino, 1859

The decisive conflict for the unification of Italy

Harold Carmichael Wylly C. B.

LEONAUR

The Campaign of Magenta and Solferino 1859:
The decisive conflict for the unification of Italy
by Harold Carmichael Wylly C. B.

First published under the titles
The Campaign of Magenta and Solferino, 1859

Leonaur is an imprint
of Oakpast Ltd

ISBN: 978-1-84677-714-1 (hardcover)
ISBN: 978-1-84677-713-4 (softcover)

http://www.leonaur.com

Publisher's Notes

In the interests of authenticity, the spellings, grammar and place names used have been retained from the original editions.

The opinions of the authors represent a view of events in which he was a participant related from his own perspective, as such the text is relevant as an historical document.

The views expressed in this book are not necessarily those of the publisher.

Contents

Preface

The campaign of 1859 in Northern Italy was one of the first of the epoch-making, rapidly conducted wars which marked the latter half of the nineteenth century. It was, moreover, as has been pointed out by the author of *Imperial Strategy*, the "first war in Europe which conveyed some preliminary indication of what railways can accomplish. The success of the French Army in this short and brilliant, if rather lucky, campaign was largely due to the efficient service of the southern railways."

A study of the events of the war and of the various considerations which led to the somewhat unexpected determination to make peace, leads one to the conviction that, while a lavish expenditure on the outbreak of war can so far repair the neglect of the years of peace and plenty that armies may be improvised for a campaign of short duration, neither hurried organisation nor makeshift armies are equal to a protracted effort, or to oppose the forces of those who have used the long years of peace to prepare for the days of war.

So far as I am aware this is the first study of the war, compiled from official sources, which has yet appeared in the English language. Several short accounts of the events of the campaign were published within a few months of its conclusion, but all these were based upon contemporary and unofficial accounts. In this short history I have followed, at a respectful distance, the general arrangement of the French official account, while I have taken the descriptions of the country and of the battlefields almost entirely from the writings of the different newspaper correspondents of that day.

H. C. W.

CHAPTER 1

Preparations for War

For centuries the nations of Europe had treated Italy as their battlefield. Swiss mercenaries, German *lanzknechts*, French and Spanish men-at-arms have all at various periods trampled Italy under foot and looked upon her as a conquered country; campaign has followed upon campaign, and in few of these have the natives of the country had any real or abiding interest, while in all of them have they most grievously suffered.

With the close of the war of the Spanish Succession, Austria became the possessor of the Spanish dominions in Italy, and, giving up the Two Sicilies to the Bourbons, ruled the smaller states of the Peninsula. By the terms of the Peace of Utrecht, Victor Amadeus II of Savoy and Piedmont had obtained Sicily; but in consequence of the attempts of Cardinal Alberoni, the Spanish Minister, to recover the lost Italian provinces, the Emperor Charles VI had insisted upon Amadeus ceding Sicily to him, and taking in exchange the Kingdom of Sardinia, and thus the title of "King of Sardinia" was borne henceforward by those who ruled in Piedmont and Savoy.

The invasions of Buonaparte shattered temporarily the power of Austria, while they introduced the teachings of the Revolution to the downtrodden peoples of Northern Italy and turned their thoughts to the "*Risorgimento*," The Kingdom of Italy, which Napoleon had created and whose crown he had assumed, fell with him, and the former governments were at once restored. The Congress of Vienna gave Lombardy and Venetia to Austria and Genoa to Savoy, while members of the House of Habsburg reigned in Parma, Modena and Tuscany. In 1831 Charles Albert became King of Sardinia, and by him the idea of a free and united Italy was fostered and encouraged.

When in 1848 the news of the revolutions in France and Austria reached Italy, Venice and Lombardy rose in revolt, drove the Austrian troops under the guns of the Quadrilateral and asked help of Piedmont. Tuscany sent troops, Ferdinand of Naples promised assistance, the Pope sent 17,000 men, and thus encouraged and supported Charles Albert took the field against the Austrians; successful at Goito, the Italians were defeated by the veteran Radetzky at Curtatone, Custoza and Novara, whereupon Charles Albert capitulated and abdicated the throne in favour of his son Victor Emmanuel.

It was the Crimean War which first gave Piedmont an opportunity of asserting herself among the nations of Europe. Count Cavour had now become Prime Minister, and it seemed to him that by intervening in so momentous a struggle, his country would acquire an increased importance among the Powers; and in spite of many difficulties he succeeded in effecting an alliance with England and France, under which 15,000 Piedmontese troops proceeded to the Crimea under General La Marmora.

At the Congress of Paris in 1856 Cavour drew attention to the danger which now threatened Italy in general, and Piedmont in particular, pointing out that the military occupation by Austria of the greater part of the Peninsula was effectually destroying the political balance of power in the various states.

In the summer of 1858 Napoleon III met Count Cavour at Plombières, where a treaty of alliance was drawn up, under which it was agreed that France should come to the assistance of Piedmont in the event of the latter being attacked by Austria. At a reception of the *Corps Diplomatique* on January 1, 1859, the Emperor of the French used the following words to the Austrian ambassador: *"Je regrette que les relations entre nous soient si mauvaises; dites cependant à votre souverain que mes sentiments pour lui ne sont pas changés"*

In face of the attitude now assumed by France and Piedmont, Austria despatched fresh troops to various points on the Piedmontese frontier, to which measures Cavour replied by asking Parliament for a special credit and by calling upon Garibaldi to raise a corps of volunteers. England and Russia now suggested that all difficulties should be laid for settlement before an international congress, to which proposal the French Emperor acceded. Austria, however, insisted that Piedmont should first disarm, and on April 23 she followed up this demand by an ultimatum to be answered within three days. On the 26th the ultimatum was rejected, and after a delay, occasioned by renewed efforts at mediation on the part of England, the Austrian troops crossed—on April 29—the frontier between Lombardy and Piedmont.

Before detailing the preparations which each of the three Powers had made and was still perfecting against the impending struggle, it may be well to offer some description of the country wherein great events were about to transpire.

That portion in which the more active part of the campaign took place lies between Turin and Mantua, and may be described in general terms as a plain, ninety miles long and thirty broad, with the River Po forming its southern boundary. It is crossed from north to south by several rivers—the majority of them with wide gravelly beds and very empty during the heats of summer; sometimes two or three channels separated by islands and sandbanks. The Po is considerably larger than any of its tributaries, and at Valenza, below its junction with the Sesia, the stream in winter is 550 yards wide.

Tracts of marshy ground, thick with bushes and trees, border the Po on either side, and the embankments, made to preserve the country from inundations, have caused the bed of the river to raise itself above the original level. In 1859 the land was very closely cultivated—vines, corn and rice—and was intersected in every direction by irrigation channels. The whole country was like one, vast orchard, being planted closely with young fruit trees, impeding the view in every direction.

Villages were numerous and each one had its cemetery beside it—square enclosures with stone walls eight to fifteen feet high, entered by an iron gate with a grated opening on either side. The roads were of three classes—*strade reale* or *postale, strade provinciale*, and *strade communale*; the first were excellent, the second good, while the third were often mere tracks, quickly becoming impassable in bad weather or under much traffic. Most of the railways were only single lines.

In view of the support, moral and material, which Napoleon had given or was pledged to afford Piedmont in her quarrel with Austria, there can be no doubt that the rapid passing of events preliminary to the outbreak of hostilities, found the French army dangerously unprepared. It is true that on January 1, 1859, the effective strength of the French forces amounted to close upon 562,000 men, but of these some 163,000 were *en congé renouvelable*; the artillery was deficient of nearly 25,000 horses, which had to be purchased between the beginning of the year and the commencement of the war; while this arm of the service was at this very time engaged in the process of rearmament with a new rifled field-gun.

The infantry was almost equally unprepared; the issue of a new rifle had, it is true, been just completed, but the arsenals contained in January—barely four months before the Austrian ultimatum reached Turin—only fourteen million rounds, which had been manufactured and stored as practice ammunition for the annual course of musketry which was to have begun in February. The stores contained clothing, equipment and camp equipage for rather less than four hundred thousand men; there was any amount of transport material in the parks at Vernon and Chateauroux, but men, horses and mules were wanting; and as late even as the beginning of April, the reserve supplies of rations and forage were wholly insufficient for the large force which might well be expected to take the field within a few days.

By immense exertions and by means of a lavish expenditure these deficiencies were in great measure made good. By recalling men to the Colours, by voluntary re-engagements, by calling in the men of the 1857 class still remaining to be incorporated and also the contingent for 1858, the total effective strength of the French Army was raised to a grand total of 639,000 men. By large purchases of remounts and by the transfer to the artillery of 4,000 men from the two other arms, the whole of the artillery of the four first corps of the Army of Italy was completely organised within twenty days; sixty batteries were to have been armed with the new rifled gun during the financial year 1859, but events marched so rapidly that the execution of this intention had perforce to be abandoned, and France eventually took the field with only thirty-two batteries armed on the new system.

Orders for a hundred million rounds of small arm ammunition were placed with different manufactories, while contracts for the soldiers' clothing, tentage and equipment were given out, and were taken up and executed with such dispatch that, on the actual outbreak of war, almost everything necessary was ready for issue to the units under orders for Italy. The Transport Department was greatly expanded in regard to personnel, while later on, during the course of the campaign, an auxiliary train of civilian *employés* with private wagons was organized and proved of the greatest service.

In regard, too, to Commissariat supplies, immense orders for biscuit were placed in London and Liverpool, while Colonel Saget, of the French General Staff, was fortunately able to arrange with the Sardinian government for seventeen days' rations for 100,000 men, with forage for 10,000 animals, to be ready stored for the use of the French troops at six different depôts on Italian soil.

Ever since the disastrous campaign of 1849 the military organization of the Kingdom of Sardinia and the development of its warlike resources had been the chief care of successive governments. The creation of the new army had been the work of the last ten anxious years; it had been entirely remodelled and had lost that exclusive class-colouring which had formerly distinguished it, and which had doubtless contributed in some degree to its failure in the last struggle with Austria.

As the Piedmontese Army was to be the nucleus round which soldiers from all parts of Italy were to group themselves, it was felt that it could not remain so exclusively aristocratic, but must be popularised, and whatever was effected in this direction was generally and justly attributed to General La Marmora. By a patient process of years a cadre was thus formed on a sufficiently broad and expansive basis to include the elements from the rest of the Peninsula in the event of an Italian war of independence.

The Kingdom was divided into five military divisions—Turin, Chambery (Savoy), Alessandria, Genoa and Cagliari (Sardinia)—and into two subdivisions—Novara and Nice. The peace strength of the army was 49,000 men with eighty guns, and it was capable of expansion to nearly 87,000 with 160 guns on the outbreak of war. This force was distributed among ninety battalions of infantry, nine regiments of cavalry and fifteen batteries, and was organised in one cavalry division and five infantry divisions, each of two brigades, the whole being under the immediate command of King Victor Emmanuel.

With the publication of the Emperor Napoleon's speech of January 1, great preparations for war were at once put in hand by the Sardinian government; supplies were hastily thrown into the fortresses of Casale and Alessandria; fortified camps were prepared; the defences of Valenza were strengthened; large purchases of animals and clothing were made; and 60,000 rifles were ordered in France to replace the smooth-bore muskets with which the Italian infantry was armed. The agitation began to spread all over the Peninsula and especially in Upper and Central Italy.

"The Italian National Society," which had been formed under Garibaldi, La Farina and Pallavicino to promote the Italian movement, had succeeded in establishing an understanding with all the most influential men, and by their exertions thousands of youths were enabled to come into Piedmont to enlist. In the month of March alone close upon 6,000 volunteers were enrolled by the commissioner specially appointed for that purpose in Turin—half of these being from Lombardy and the remainder from Central Italy, and altogether it is computed that some 14,500 men were voluntarily enlisted.

The Piedmontese were no match single-handed for the large forces which Austria had already ranged—or was in process of concentrating—upon their eastern frontier. It was therefore necessary to take up some strong defensive position wherein they could await the arrival of the French troops, which, on the declaration of war, would at once begin to arrive in Piedmont, either by Susa through and over the passes of the Alps or by sea by way of Toulon and Genoa. General Niel, *aide-de-camp* to the Emperor of the French, had been sent early to Turin to concert measures of defence with General La Marmora, and by them it was decided that a position should be taken up on the right bank of the Dora Baltea, between the village of Mazze and the Po, as it was considered that the Austrians would be unlikely to risk an advance on Turin from the east, but would more probably move on the capital by Vercelli, threatening at the same time the *débouchés* of the French columns from the Alps. The Italian forces were consequently thus disposed:

One division covering the valley of the Scrivia and Genoa.

One division occupying Alessandria.

One division occupying Casale, watching the line of the Po at Valenza and maintaining communication between Casale and Alessandria; this distribution thus left only two infantry divisions, the cavalry and Garibaldi's corps to oppose the passage of the Dora Baltea. It was hoped, however, that the march of the Austrians from the Ticino might be so delayed as to extend over five or six days, by which time the French Army—debouching rapidly from the passes of the Alps and using the two available lines of railway—might well be able to place the best part of three divisions in line with the Piedmontese.

The Austrian Army—having a peace strength of 334,000 and

a strength on a war footing of 720,000—was organised in four armies and twelve corps: at the end of 1858 the Second Army—strength 44,837 men with 104 guns—under Count Gyulai, formed the normal garrison of Northern Italy, with the 5th, 7th and 8th Corps, of which it was composed, occupying Milan, Verona and Padua respectively. The infantry was in process of rearmament with a new rifle, but only a small number of these had been issued and many units did not receive the new weapon until actually on the march to the theatre of war.

Already in November, 1858, matters were beginning to assume so threatening an aspect, that it was decided to raise the strength of the Second Army to 76,000 men with 200 guns, and further to arrange for the dispatch to Italy at short notice of the 3rd Corps, but on a peace footing only, taking steps, however, for increasing the number of the effectives of these four corps to a total of 170,000 men at ten weeks' notice. Gyulai represented that such a force was quite inadequate to guard against all possible eventualities, and reminded the War Ministry that similar half-measures in 1848 had obliged his predecessor Radetzky temporarily to loosen his hold upon Lombardy. These representations were, however, disregarded, and the Ministry proceeded to carry out the scheme already suggested, The 3rd Corps was moved to Italy early in January, and on its arrival the following was the disposition of the four Austrian corps:—

The 5th Corps, with one brigade of the 3rd, between the Ticino and the Adda;
The 7th Corps between the Mincio and the Adige;
The 8th Corps in the Legations and in Venetia; while of the remaining brigades of the 3rd Corps one was in Brescia, one in Bergamo, one in Cremona and one in Lodi and Crema.[1]
On February 15 the 2nd Corps followed the 3rd to Italy and arrived in Milan on March 3.

It now appearing to be inevitable that Austria would, in the

---

1. At this period the 3rd Corps contained five brigades.

event of war, have to deal both with France and Piedmont, orders were issued on April 5 and 6 for the five corps already in Italy to be at once brought up to war strength, and on the 13th the 9th Corps also left Vienna for the front.

Towards the latter end of April the five corps (2nd, 3rd, 5th, 7th and 8th), already standing ready behind the Ticino, were made up as follows:

Army Corps.	Divs.	Brigades.	Batts.	Squadrons.	Guns.
2nd ...	2	4	20		40
3rd ...	2	4	24	8	56
5th ...	2	5	24	8	64
7th ...	2	4	18	4	48
8th ...	2	4	20	4	48
Reserves					
1 Infantry Division		3	14	3½	28
1 Cavalry Division		2		24	16
Artillery.					116

12 divisions. 26 brigades. 120 battalions. 51½ squadrons. 416 guns.

There were also 46 battalions of occupation or garrison troops, with a few guns and a small body of cavalry.

The total strength of the Austrian forces in the Peninsula amounted to nearly 230,000 men, but from this total some 70,000 must be deducted, required for the maintenance of order and for garrison duty in the Austrian possessions in Italy, leaving barely 160,000 men available to take the offensive beyond the frontier.

On April 25 the Imperial forces were thus distributed: the 2nd Corps between S. Angiolo and Lodi, the 3rd Corps at Pavia, the 5th between Pavia and Milan, the 7th between Bereguardo and Abbiategrasso on the Ticino, and the 8th at Piacenza. The two brigades of the Cavalry Division were in Crema and Manerbio, while of the Reserve Infantry Division, one brigade was on its way to join the 2nd Corps and the other two were in Brescia and Bologna.

On April 27, reports were received at Austrian Headquarters that French ships had already arrived in Genoa, that the disembarkation of men and material was proceeding rapidly, and that French troops were marching to Italy through Savoy. Gyulai had already arranged for the violation of the frontier to commence on the 30th, but on the morning of the 29th these orders were cancelled and the passage of the Ticino was at once begun by the 7th and 5th Corps at Bereguardo, while the 3rd, 8th and 2nd, concentrating at Pavia, crossed the river by the stone bridge at that town and by pontoons which had previously been thrown across.

By night on the 30th practically the whole of Austria's striking force had arrived upon hostile territory.

CHAPTER 2

The Austrian Advance to the Sesia

In the meantime the French had quietly, but with dispatch, continued their preparations for placing their army upon a war footing and for holding it in readiness for an immediate advance.

A large number of the veteran troops quartered in Africa were ordered to be transferred to France, their places being taken by less experienced soldiers, and eight divisions of infantry and one of cavalry were standing ready by the middle of April, behind the Alps or between Lyons and the sea, to advance into Italy through the mountain passes or by sea to Genoa. By April 21 the French Government had fully made up its mind as to the hostile intentions of Austria, and on that date orders were issued for the formation of four army corps which, with the Imperial Guard, were to be known as "the Army of the Alps"—a title almost immediately altered to that of "the Army of Italy." Of this army the Emperor Napoleon III himself took command, while the subordinate commands were filled as follows:—

The Imperial Guard—General Regnaud de Saint Jean d'Angély;
The 1st Army Corps—Marshal Count Baraguey d'Hilliers;
The 2nd Army Corps—General de MacMahon;
The 3rd Army Corps—Marshal Canrobert; and the 4th Corps—General Niel. The command of the artillery was held by General le Boeuf, and that of the engineers by

General Frossard. The 3rd and 4th Corps were directed to move into Italy by the Alps, while the two divisions of the Imperial Guard and the 1st and 2nd Corps were ordered to Marseilles and Toulon for embarkation for Genoa. The 2nd Corps was very largely composed of troops serving in Africa, whose transfer to French soil had not yet been quite completed, and these were consequently ordered to proceed direct to Genoa from Algerian ports.

Of the available cavalry one division was attached to the 1st and another to the 3rd Corps, while to the 2nd and 4th a brigade each only was allotted.

On April 25 the following movements were initiated; the division Bouat of Canrobert's Corps was entrained at Lyons, reached railhead at St. Jean de Maurienne, and by the 28th had crossed the Mont Cenis and debouched at Susa.[1] Bourbaki's Division of the same corps was directed on Briançon, and ordered to move at once into Piedmont, and by the 28th Ducrot's Brigade of that division had surmounted the Mont Genévre. On the 25th the division Renault of the 3rd Corps marched on Montmelian in the direction of Mont Cenis. The 4th Corps followed close behind the 3rd and was succeeded by the cavalry of both.

The movements by sea were executed with equal rapidity. Bazaine's Division of the 1st Corps was already on the 29th beginning to disembark at Genoa; the divisions Ladmirault and Forey were put on board the transports as fast as they reached Toulon and Marseilles, as were also the troops of the Imperial Guard arriving at these ports from Paris, while transports were working between Genoa and the Algerian ports conveying the matured soldiers of the Army of Africa. The cavalry division of the Guard, having been trained from Paris to Marseilles, followed thence by march route the Corniche road to Genoa.

While these various movements were in course of execution, the formation of a 5th Corps was undertaken; this was

---

1. Bouat died almost immediately of sunstroke and was succeeded by Trochu.

placed under the orders of Prince Napoleon, and the two divisions of which it was composed were commanded by Generals D'Autemarre and Uhrich. The 1st Division was entirely made up of troops from the African garrisons, while the 2nd was formed of regiments from Paris.

In preparing for a campaign beyond the frontiers of the Empire, it was imperative that the defence of the country, whence so large a force was to be withdrawn, should be neither neglected nor overlooked. To keep order in the interior of France and to safeguard her borders the following dispositions were made: Marshal de Castellane was placed in command of three infantry divisions—one at Besançon and two—with a cavalry division—at Lyons; Marshal Magnan was at the head of four divisions of infantry, of which two were in Paris, one at Lille and one at Mézières; while Marshal Pélissier, Duke de Malakoff, united under his command four divisions of infantry and four of cavalry, which were dispersed in Chalons, Metz, Lunéville and Strasbourg.

It must be admitted that if the near approach of war found the armies of France in great measure unprepared for a struggle with her ancient foe, extraordinarily successful efforts had been made within the course of a month to atone for the perilous condition of unreadiness to which the country had been permitted to relapse after the termination of the Crimean War. Experience has over and over again taught nations and individuals that the neglected work of years cannot be made good in a few feverish days when war is imminent; in many respects the French armies were anything but thoroughly equipped for a stern campaign, but the fact remains that in something like twenty-five days an army of 100,000 men of all arms had been collected in France and in Algeria and set down in Piedmont, ready, so far as the casual observer could judge, for all the exigencies of war.

It will be noticed that while the advance of the Austrians on the 29th—when they crossed the frontier between Lombardy and Piedmont—actually opened the campaign, the first infringement of existing treaties came from France, whose troops advanced into Savoy on the 25th. Some days, however, before that date, it was known that war was inevitable; it is true that Austria's ultimatum was not presented in Turin before the 23rd, but to the parties most nearly concerned its contents was well known as early as the 21st.

The result made itself felt; before the memorandum was even presented, the railway had carried French troops to the Piedmontese frontier, while many thousand soldiers were concentrated in Toulon and Marseilles. Ten steamers of the *Messageries* were lying in the Joliette Harbour ready to take troops on board; a number of old paddle-wheel ships converted into transports were moored close by. Several line-of-battle ships and large transports were already on their way to fetch the African divisions, while other ships, chartered for the conveyance of stores, were loading with the utmost expedition.

Thus, if in the ultimatum a time-limit, not of three days but of twenty-four hours, had been fixed, the French divisions, having already had a day's start, would have still been in Piedmont at the end of the shorter period. By the 26th, when the time fixed by the ultimatum had expired, the French had had full five days to prepare, and before the Austrian envoy left Turin with Cavour's reply, French troops already stood upon Italian soil.

At the moment of advance the French Army was divided into two great wings with no prospect of reunion or support until each had arrived in Piedmont. The left wing, composed of the 3rd and 4th Corps, was therefore placed temporarily under the command of Marshal Canrobert, while the right wing—the 1st and 2nd Corps—was under the orders of Marshal Baraguey d'Hilliers. The two forts of Exiles and of Esseillon command respectively the eastern exits of the passes of Mont Genévre and Mont Cenis, and, by arrangement with King Victor Emmanuel, these were handed over to mixed garrisons of French and Italian troops.

Having set in motion the troops of the left wing, which was ordered to concentrate at Turin and thence to march by divisions to the position on the Dora Baltea, Marshal Canrobert left Lyons on April 27, accompanied by General Niel, the commander of the 4th Corps, reached Susa on the night of the 28th and Turin the following day, and moved out at once from here to the Dora Baltea with King Victor Emmanuel and Generals Niel and Frossard. Having carefully examined the ground, the Marshal came to the conclusion that owing to its extent, to the small numbers available for holding it, and to the configuration of the ground itself, the position was not specially favourable for defence.

On the right the position was good; flanked by the River Po, there lay beyond the Dora Baltea an open plain completely dominated by the fire of guns placed on the right bank. In the rear of the right the ground was very broken, and covered with houses, trees and hedges, assisting greatly in the defence; a village called Verolengo was itself strongly entrenched and could only be forced with great difficulty, while this village, with that of Terrazza, stood out like two bastions connected by a canal as by a curtain.

The left at Mazze was on a hill commanding the ground to the front and too precipitous for frontal assault. In front again the bed of the Dora, enclosed between two high banks quite 2,000 yards apart, also assisted in the defence of the position selected by the Sardinians; while the railway, running parallel to the course of the river, permitted of reinforcements being brought up to any portion of the line which might be threatened. Such were the considerations which had influenced the Italians in the choice of the position wherein to await the advance of the Austrians; but the following serious defects were pointed out by Marshal Canrobert.

The town of Rondissone formed the centre of the position; the high road from Turin to Milan ran through it, and the ground in rear—flat and open—offered no obstacle where an enemy might be detained or defenders rallied. If the centre were forced the right would be turned, the left compromised, and the second line would be taken in reverse. Lastly the river, the only obstacle covering Rondissone, here formed several small channels almost everywhere fordable at that season of the year; the banks also were thickly wooded and precipitous. Then, too, although the left was strong, it could easily be turned by the Austrians following the high road, which crossed the river twelve miles north of Mazze.

Such were the faults of the position, but it is possible that none the less it would have been retained, had the 3rd and 4th French Corps been able to join hands with their allies as early as had been anticipated. The weather, however, had been deplorable, and the passage of the Alps had been so greatly delayed, that, should the Austrians only march rapidly on the Dora Baltea, there seemed no prospect of reinforcing the defenders with anything but very weak detachments of the French left wing.

These considerations led Marshal Canrobert to ask that the position on the Dora be abandoned, and that Turin should be defended at Alessandria and Casale, since the occupation in force of the last-named place in particular, might cause anxiety to the Austrian commander for his left and for his communications in the event of his advance by way of Vercelli. Thus, too, the capital would be covered, Genoa safeguarded, the unmolested arrival of the French detachments would be assured and the junction of the allied armies be placed beyond danger.

These ideas of Marshal Canrobert were approved by the King and by the Emperor, and the position on the Dora Baltea, where La Marmora had already constructed important defensive works, was definitely abandoned. By the use of the railway the troops were rapidly withdrawn, and under the direction of General Frossard works were begun on the left bank of the Po at Casale, in the hope of thereby causing Count Gyulai to believe that an advance was contemplated against his left flank should he march on Turin.

In consequence of these dispositions the following alterations took place in the positions of the Italian forces:—

Royal Headquarters at San Salvatore.
1st Division (Castelborgo) at San Salvatore.
2nd   ,,   (Fanti)   at Alessandria.

3rd	„	(Durando)	at Valenza.
4th	„	Cialdini)	at Giarole.
5th	„	(Cucchiari)	at Casale and Frassineto.

The Cavalry Division, with two batteries of horse artillery, remained on the Dora Baltea, forming the extreme left and observing the Austrian right, and occupied the villages of Cigliano, Mandria di Chivasso and Rondissone.

On the date when operations should have commenced, it had been reported in Milan that the Italian forces were still not concentrated, and it was clear therefore that Austria's best chance of success in the coming campaign lay in striking hard and expeditiously. To cross into the Lomellina—as the southern portion of the country between the Sesia and the Ticino is called—was not the only line of advance open to Count Gyulai; he could have advanced either by the north or by the south bank of the Po— the one led to the capital, the other to the enemy's forces and lines of communication.

It is interesting, therefore, to study the memorandum prepared by the Austrian General Staff and dated April 20, of which the following are extracts:

The military situation may shortly be summed up as follows: our enemies in the first line are Sardinians, in the second the French. The Sardinians, 60,000 strong, having been somewhat abruptly disturbed in their military preparations and plans, have a double object in view: first, to preserve intact their capital; second, to secure their army from defeat until the arrival of the French. Probably they will consider that both of these objects are not to be attained, and, having to select, will possibly prefer to sacrifice Turin for a time, in the general interests of the war, to exposing their army to an unequal contest in its defence, which may entail its destruction.

It is to be feared, therefore, that the Sardinian forces will be found concentrating under shelter of their fortresses on the strong ground south of the Po, with the further purpose of covering the defiles and communications between Genoa and Alessandria. Should this anticipation not be realised—should the Sardinians have divided their forces in pursuit of a double objective and should they have preferred to concentrate on the Dora Baltea, which river has recently been prepared for defence, with a view to cover Turin directly—the problem to be solved by the Imperial Army will be considerably simplified.

In either of these cases, assuming the Sardinian Army to be inferior in numbers as well as in quality, the decisive result of early collision would seem still more certain than if the remedy for inferiority were sought by enlisting such artificial aid as is presented by the permanent fortifications south of the Po. On the other hand it may be safely assumed that every nerve will be strained by the French to arrive sufficiently early on Sardinian soil to support their allies in the impending struggle.

Assuming that our ultimatum will on delivery be immediately telegraphed to Paris, it may be calculated that the French will move within twenty-four hours from that time; and considering further the character of the communications across the Alps on one hand, and the difficulty attending the maritime transport of so large a body of men on the other—though the distance does not exceed three hundred miles—we may safely calculate that the Sardinians, unless they retire on Genoa or Susa, will, during the first six days, be entirely unsupported, and that in no probable case will our operations be exposed to serious danger from the arrival of the French—under proper precautions—for a fortnight at least.

Assuming, therefore, that our proper objective must be sought in the Sardinian Army, and not in the Sardinian capital, in the first instance, from considerations precisely similar to those which influence our adversary, the question is how best to utilize the time at our disposal for the purpose in view—the destruction of the Sardinian Army.

It would seem advisable that the advance upon the position presumed to be occupied by the enemy should be made by both banks of the Po; the army thus operating a cheval along the river, with a view to secure the passages as we proceed and to enlist the largest possible number of communications for the rapid transit of our forces towards the objective.

The first objective points, marking the earliest phase of the operations, are Valenza and Tortona. It is deemed essential that the permanent passage at the former town should be seized at once, and if the bridge be destroyed or impaired, steps taken to restore immediate communication with the north bank of the Po. The construction of works on the south bank of the river will be commenced at once.

If the enemy stands here, dispositions for attack should be issued to the army. If he prefers to cling to the high ground about Occimiano, the passage of the river will be effected and the 2nd and 3rd Corps will cross at Valenza to the south bank.

It may be expected that Valenza will pass into the hands of the Imperial Army on the 28th and Tortona on the 29th. On the 30th or 31st at latest the army should be concentrated for attack on the Sardinians in a probably entrenched position. ... It may be estimated that the Imperial Army may reach the Sardinian capital about May 3, and further operations would then be dictated by circumstances which cannot now be foreseen.

In case of repulse at Occimiano, the army would retire upon Valenza, where the necessary preparations for its retreat to the north bank will have been made . . . and the army generally would take up a defensive position in the Lomellina, holding the passages of the Po and Sesia, and leaning with its right upon Vercelli, which should be strengthened for that purpose.

It will be seen from the above that the Austrian General Staff had formed a tolerably correct appreciation of the situation likely to arise out of an outbreak of war, and of the best means of dealing with it; the want of decision apparent in the movements about to be described is therefore the more inexplicable.

In spite of the fact that on April 25 Count Gyulai telegraphed to Vienna his determination to remain purely on the defensive, in view of the approaching concentration of the French and Italian armies, the Austrian forces continued to advance westwards after crossing the Ticino.

On the night of the 30th the outpost line was on the river Terdoppio, the 8th Corps being at Cava—Zinasco—Piave d'Albignola—Corana; the 2nd at Gropello; the 7th at Gambolo—Vigevano; the 5th at Gariasco—Trumello; and the 3rd Corps at Dorno, while the Cavalry remained in Pavia. Orders were given to the engineers to fortify the line of the Gravellone stream, to bridge it in several places, to improve all approaches to the several crossings of the Ticino, to lay a semi-permanent bridge at Vigevano, and to prepare bridgeheads at Vigevano and San Martino—on the Milan-Trecate-Novara road. (The bridgehead prepared at Vigevano consisted of five separate field works, while that at San Martino comprised three *lunettes*.)

On May 1 Army Headquarters was at Gariasco and the Austrians moved forward to the line of the Agogna—the 8th Corps being at San Nazzaro, the 3rd at Lomello and Ferrara, the 2nd at San Giorgio, the 5th at Mortara, and the 7th between Albonese and Cilavegna. The commander of the last-named corps caused two squadrons and two companies to be pushed on to Novara, where a requisition for 100,000 rations was made and complied with, and where a number of maps were seized. This day the Cavalry Division got no further than Trumello on the Terdoppio.

Urban, commanding the Reserve Division, sent a brigade to Barlassina on the Milan-Como road, owing to the reported irruption of Italian Free troops into Lombardy from that direction.

On this date Gyulai was informed that in a fortnight's time another corps would be dispatched to the scene of operations.

On May 2 the advance was continued until the Imperial Army stood on the line of the Sesia, the different corps being distributed as follows: the 8th at Piave de Cairo, the 3rd at Torre dei Beretti, the 5th at Candia, the 7th occupying San Angelo—Robbio—Palestro—Torrione—Rosasco, sending an advanced post to Vercelli and reconnoitring the roads towards Trino and Casale; the 2nd Corps was at Mede, and Army Headquarters at Lomello.

This day one of Urban's brigades arrived in Como, being supported by a battalion in Barlassina.

In front of the 8th and 5th Corps only were any of the enemy to be seen; the weather, which had been favourable at the commencement of the advance, had now changed again for the worse, and the Sesia was greatly swollen.

Count Gyulai issued for May 3 march orders of which the general object is anything but clear. The 8th Corps was directed to send troops on to the island opposite Cambioin the hope that the Allies would believe that an attempt was to be made to cross the Po at Sale and at Porto Cornale, while the 5th Corps was to make demonstrations at different points along the Sesia and Po, in order to delude the enemy into the belief that a crossing might be attempted at Frassinetto, It would seem that the idea of all these movements and demonstrations was to cover a real attempt to cross the Po in the direction of Alessandria.

At Army Headquarters it was intended that the 3rd Corps should seize the bridge at Valenza, and that another should at the same time be thrown across at Bassignana; the 2nd Corps, followed by the 8th, was to pass over the river here, while the 3rd, 5th and 7th crossed at Valenza. These corps were then to assault and capture the heights of San Salvatore, and having effected the overthrow of the Italian Army would then press on against the French.

Early in the morning the artillery of the 3rd Corps opened fire against Valenza, but the commander, Count Schwartzenberg, seems to have been doubtful in regard to his orders, for we find him writing to Army Headquarters to inquire whether the railway bridge was to be captured or merely destroyed. The 5th Corps only received its orders at 5.30 a.m., and the commander then pointed out that both rivers were so full that it would be no easy matter to send even cavalry across; that all boats had been removed by the enemy; and that it would be difficult to make a realistic feint of crossing when no bridging material of any kind was on his charge.

By midday, however, the Sesia had fallen and was crossed in several places by Paumgartten's division, which pushed on to Villanova, Terranuova and Caresana, leading to some sharp skirmishing. At Cambio and Cornale troops of the 8th Corps were also put across the Po in pontoons, but saw few signs of the enemy.

On this date a bridge and bridgehead were commenced at Vaccarizza below Pavia, which were intended, in the event of a future retirement on Pavia, to cover the communications and protect the passage of the army over the river. Vercelli was occupied by the 7th Corps with outposts on the Casale and Trino roads.

Urban had returned this day to Brescia by rail, but on receipt of intelligence that the Parma government had been overturned, he was ordered to proceed to that city and restore order.

Previous to crossing the Ticino the Austrian commander-in-chief had received vague reports as to the dispatch and arrival in Italy of the leading French troops, but it was not until May 3—at an hour when Count Gyulai had already issued his orders for the demonstrations on the Po and Sesia—that he was in receipt of telegraphic despatches from Vienna informing him that—"fifty thousand Frenchmen had been directed on Casale and Alessandria on May 1"—"that Bouat's division had already arrived in Turin over the Mont Cenis"—"that 10,000 men were being daily forwarded *via* Toulon, 8,000 *via* Marseilles and 7,000 *via* Brianyon"—and it was doubtless in consequence of these reports that Gyulai telegraphed to Vienna on the evening of the 3rd that "the approach of the French prevented his intention of breaking through at Bassignana."

The 3rd Corps (Schwartzenberg) was accordingly directed to destroy the bridge at Valenza, but the rain was now very heavy, the rising water drowned the mines which had been already prepared, and the destruction of the bridge was delayed for several days.

On the 4th Gyulai learnt that the 9th Corps was being sent into Italy; this had, at the outbreak of war, been employed in the protection of the Adriatic littoral, and on May 10 its transport to Italy via Venice commenced, one brigade moving daily. Its place was taken by the 10th Corps from Vienna.

Early on the morning of the 4th the Brigade Boer of the 8th Corps crossed the Po at Porto Comale without opposition, and at once commenced the construction of a pontoon bridge. The remaining three brigades followed, Castelnuova was occupied, and parties were sent forward in the direction of Voghera, Ponte Curone and Tortona, while the Corps Headquarters was established at Cecosa. It had been intended that Ponte Curone should be occupied in force, but the heavy rain, which had now been falling continuously for fifteen hours, had thrown many obstacles in the way of forward movement; later in the day, however, the Brigade Philippovic sent a small force towards Voghera to destroy the rail and telegraph, while arrangements were also made for a mixed force (one battalion, one squadron, and two guns) to proceed next day to Tortona, there to levy requisitions. To support the 8th Corps, the 2nd was moved, half to San Nazzaro and half to Lomello.

The stream had risen so much in front of the 5th Corps at Frassinetto that the fords were rapidly becoming impassably, and Count Stadion accordingly recalled the whole of his troops to the left bank.

Of the 7th Corps a whole division was now concentrated in Vercelli; one squadron of the mounted troops with this corps was at Villate and another at Novara.

Late at night orders were issued from Gyulai's Headquarters for entirely fresh dispositions on the morrow, but no hint was vouchsafed of the reasons for any change or of the purpose for which it was made; in the orders, however, given to the 8th Corps (Benedek) it was remarked that the commander-in-chief "proposed to move with the rest of the army from the line of operations Pavia—Lomello and to take up that of Milan—Vercelli."

The 8th Corps—to which the Brigade Lippert of the 2nd Corps was attached—was to cover the left wing of the army during the operations now impending, commence the construction of a bridgehead at Porto Cornale, and at the same time push out parties towards Sale, Tortona, Ponte Curone and Voghera, and prevent information of the Austrian movements leaking through to the enemy.

The main portion of the Imperial Army was ordered to move as follows on May 5: the whole of the 7th Corps was to concentrate in Vercelli, occupy San Germano and Stroppiana, each with half a brigade, and send forward strong parties towards Desana, Biella and the line of the Dora Baltea. Vercelli was to be prepared for defence, and the local authorities were to be required to supply 110,000 rations daily; work on the bridgehead at San Martino was to be continued; while the 5th Corps was to move to Robbio, the 3rd to Candia and Cozzo, and the 2nd to Mortara and Cergnago. All bridging materials and pontoons—less five pontoons left at Cornale—were to reach Lomello on the 5th and Mortara on the 6th. Supplies for the 8th Corps were to be forwarded *via* Pavia and San Nazzaro—for the rest of the army by Milan and Novara.

The floods on the Po destroyed the bridge which had been laid at Cornale and still prevented the destruction of the railway bridge at Valenza, so that early on the morning of the 5th the orders already issued for the move towards the Dora Baltea were cancelled, but the commander of the 8th Corps was directed that, in the event of any hostile advance before communication was restored, he should retire on Piacenza, eventually rejoining the main army through Pavia.

Nothing further was to be done in regard to the bridgehead at Cornale, but every possible means was to be taken to deceive the enemy as to the isolated situation of the 8th Corps. In these circumstances Benedek showed himself very active, sending requisitions into Tortona and destroying the telegraph line and two bridges over the Scrivia near that town.

By the morning of the 6th the river had fallen considerably, and by 2.30 p.m. communication between the north and south bank was restored, when the troops commenced their retirement. By 11 p.m. all the 8th Corps had recrossed and occupied Piave de Cairo, Mezzanabigli and San Nazzaro, the 2nd Corps evacuating the last-named place and occupying Cergnago and San Giorgio.

The following movements took place on the 7th: one division of the 7th Corps took up the line San Germane—Cascine di Stra—Desana—Asigliano—Pertengo—Stroppiana, the remainder being concentrated in Vercelli. Mortara and Novara were sufficiently fortified to prevent their falling by a *coup de main*.

The 5th Corps held from Rosasco to Confienza through Robbio; the Headquarters of the 3rd Corps proceeded to Cozzo, having its brigades at S.Paolo, Leria, Celpenchio and Candia. The enemy appeared in some force about Valenza and Monte and their artillery came into action. The 2nd Corps moved to Nicorvo. This day the bulk of the 8th Corps marched to Mortara, but the brigade Lippert, detached from the 2nd Corps, was, with one of the brigades of the 8th Corps, placed under the orders of General Lang, who, with his Headquarters at Lomello, was directed to watch the line of the Po from Mezzana Corti to Breme and give timely notice of any hostile advance in the direction of Piacenza. In the event of the Allies crossing the river in strength in his front, Lang was to retire on Mortara and there make a stand to cover the left flank of the army.

The bridge at Vaccarizza was now ready, but the bad weather had seriously hindered the completion of the bridgehead.

The communication and supply lines of the different units of the army were again altered as follows: For Lang's division— Pavia—San Nazzaro—Lomello; for the 2nd and 3rd Corps— Abbiategrasso—Vigevano—Mortara; for the remainder of the army—Magenta—Novara.

On May 8 the 7th Corps pushed a brigade on from San Germano to Tronzano, but beyond this it was found that the roads leading west and north had been cut, while the bridge over the Dora Baltea was said to have been mined. Various reports of the presence of the enemy were received; a thousand horse were said to be in front of Tronzano; 25,000 Frenchmen were reported to be in Biella, while the Emperor of the French and the King of Italy were believed to be at Rondissone on the Dora Baltea with Durando's division—which last, however, was at this moment actually in Valenza. A strong patrol was sent on to Biella and parties to Ivrea, and from their reports it was clear that the Allies were in no strength in this neighbourhood.

The Brigade Gablentz of the 7th Corps sent a small force of all arms to reconnoitre the bridgehead at Casale, and this engaged the troops holding it and exploded a magazine in the works; the bridgehead was at the time held by six battalions. In support of the 3rd and 7th Corps, the 2nd moved from Nicorvo via Robbio to Vercelli, where it bivouacked south of the town. The 5th Corps—whose mission it was to destroy the railway between Vercelli and Casale—crossed the Sesia at Palestro and occupied the line Asigliano—Caresana with a brigade at Costanzana.

The 3rd Corps—less a small mixed force left to connect with Lang's division and watch the Sesia from its junction with the Po to Mantie—marched to Torrione. The 8th Corps moved to Robbio, arriving, however, very late, owing to its line of march crossing that of the 2nd and 3rd Corps at Robbio and Nicorvo.

The arches of the bridge at Valenza were this day at last destroyed.

On this day Count Gyulai both wrote and telegraphed to Urban, directing him to make a strong demonstration in the direction of Stradella with the object of drawing off the attention of the enemy in front of the main army, and of obtaining information as to the strength and dispositions of the Allies in the mountains to the southwest of that town. Urban was, however, enjoined on no account to lose sight of the fact that his main duty was to maintain order in Lombardy and Venetia, and that he was not to move far from his base at Pavia or from the nearly completed bridgehead at Vaccarizza. Gyulai concluded by remarking that, while he was tolerably certain that the main force of the enemy was concentrated about Alessandria, and although he was satisfied as to the efficacy of the steps he had taken for the security of his left flank, still a hostile movement on Pavia would be so useful to the enemy that everything possible must be done to hinder or prevent any such attempt.

In the orders for the 9th—issued at 8.30 the previous evening—it had been directed that the 7th Corps should concentrate about San Germano with outposts in Santhia and Tronzono and with patrols pushed still further westward; that the 5th Corps should move to Tricerro with advanced troops in Trino and towards Casale, and that the 2nd, 3rd, and 8th Corps should support these movements. Lang was also ordered to cross the Po in strength and endeavour to clear up the situation about Voghera.

These movements were actually in progress on the morning of the 9th, when fresh orders were issued cancelling all advance and directing the retirement of the different corps behind the Sesia, and by evening the whole of the troops—with the exception of the 5th Corps—were across that river.

In justification of this sudden retrograde movement, Count Gyulai forwarded to Vienna a long dispatch dated the 9th, of which the following is an epitome: he commenced by reiterating the words of his letter of April 25 wherein he had stated his conviction that an energetic offensive in the direction of Alessandria was very difficult in view of the strength of the allied forces—while a reverse would entail very serious consequences; that the offensive could only be undertaken to prevent or delay a junction of the French and Italian armies; and that such a consummation was only possible had the Austrians been in sufficient force to hold the Italians to the defences at Alessandria and at the same time to engage and defeat the French. A permanent separation of the Allies was impracticable, as a junction could easily take place further west, when the French could have advanced from Turin by Vercelli and Novara against Milan—a movement which Gyulai could not have prevented and which would have necessitated a retirement on Piacenza or even further. This retreat, moreover, by the right bank of the Po on a single road, with all the *impedimenta* of a large army and with possible insurrection on the flank in Tuscany, would have presented immense difficulties and would have taken a long time to carry out.

Directly the French appeared upon the scene, Gyulai stated that he became convinced any offensive against Alessandria must be abandoned, and that he must take up some position to cover Lombardy and prevent a hostile advance on Piacenza. Such a position he claimed to have discovered between Mortara and Vercelli, where, moreover, the army was spread over a fertile province. The enemy's advance would either be restricted to a very narrow front between the Po and the Apennines, or to a crossing of the river where the Austrians could fall upon and crush him during the movement.

After detailing the orders he had given for the 9th—described as a "reconnaissance" (by four army corps), Gyulai concludes his despatch by saying he has just heard that the Dora Baltea line has been abandoned on his moving in that direction, and that the French are advancing on Alessandria to threaten Piacenza; that consequently his previous orders for a westward move have been cancelled, and that the corps have been directed to concentrate about Mortara where he proposes to await developments.

CHAPTER 3

Action at Montebello

While the events were transpiring which have been described in the latter part of the preceding chapter, the different portions of the French Army had gradually and unhindered been drawing closer to their allies.

By May 1 three French corps—including that under the command of Prince Napoleon—had already disembarked at Genoa, and one of these—the 1st—was on its way to Novi *via* Staglieno, Pontedecimo and Voltaggio. Of the two corps moving into Piedmont through the passes of the Alps, the 3rd was already strung out along the line Susa—Turin—Alessandria, while the head of the other was across the mountains. On the 2nd the 1st Corps was at Pontedecimo, Buzzola, Voltaggio and Serravalle; the 2nd was at Bolzanetto, San Quilico and Campomarone; the Imperial Guard was at Genoa while Trochu's division of the 3rd Corps reached Alessandria on this date.

The Italian Headquarters was still at San Salvatore, the 1st Division was at Occimiano and Valenza, the 2nd and 3rd were in Alessandria, the 4th in Ozzano, and the 5th in Frassinetto, Valenza and Bassignana. On May 3 Garibaldi's Free Corps arrived in Casale, he having been earnestly entreated by Cialdini to come there with all speed, as the advance of the Austrian 5th Corps had caused Cialdini anxiety for the safety of his bridge defences.

On the 4th the 1st French Corps was at Rigoroso, Arquato and Serravalle; the 2nd at Gavi, Carosio and Voltaggio; the 3rd was partly in Turin and partly in Alessandria, while the 4th was still between Susa and the capital.

The French were gradually closing up during the ensuing days, until on the 7th the head of the 1st Corps—marching on the right bank of the Scrivia—had reached Cassano; the Imperial Guard following had arrived at Buzzola; the 2nd Corps was at Tasserolo just south of Novi; and the 3rd and 4th Corps were both in Alessandria, less one brigade which the last-named corps had dropped at Susa.

Some slight changes had been made in the dispositions of the Piedmontese Army; the 1st Division was in San Salvatore, the 3rd on the line Valenza—Mugarone—Bassignana, covering Alessandria, where was the 2nd Division; while the 4th and 5th were between Frassinetto and Monte, covering Casale.

The French military authorities had been thoroughly alive, not only to the evil moral effect of a hostile occupation of Turin even of a few days' duration, but of the resultant danger of the interruption of communications between Susa and Alessandria; it must therefore have been with equal astonishment and relief that the Allies heard on the 9th that the Austrians had suddenly withdrawn the bulk of their troops behind the Sesia. By the 13th the Austrians had all returned by forced marches to the Lomellina, occupying ground between the Sesia and the Ticino; the 3rd and 7th Corps were on the Sesia—the latter still holding Vercelli—the 8th was on the Po, the 2nd and 5th in rear at Albonese and Trumello.

Urban alone, with troops of the Reserve Division, was on the south bank of the Po at Casteggio, while Piacenza was left to its own garrison and to the 9th Corps, which was now drawing near to that city. Meanwhile the Allies were rapidly concentrating in two strong masses on either side of the Tanaro—the 1st, 2nd and 3rd French Corps in Sale, Voghera and Tortona, the 4th and Sardinians about Casale and Valenza, and the Imperial Guard at Alessandria, bridges having been thrown across the Scrivia and the Tanaro to facilitate inter-communication.

The first phase of the campaign had thus ended without initial advantage to the Austrians. The object of Gyulai's hasty invasion of Piedmont was less the defeat of the isolated Italian Army, than the capture of the capital and the possible overthrow of the French detachments debouching from the passes of the Alps.

But such an operation exposed the Austrian flank to attack by the armies disembarking at Genoa, and there can be no doubt that the true object of the invasion should have been the defeat of the Italian Army standing behind the Po and the Tanaro. The Austrian advance, instead of being by the left bank of the Po, should have been by the right; a force should have occupied the defiles of the Scrivia and observed Alessandria—thus checking the French advance from Genoa—and the bulk of the Austrian Army should have forced the passage of the Tanaro, and, having defeated the Italians, would then have stood ready to deal with the divided forces of their allies.

But while the Piedmontese divisions still stood unsupported, Gyulai evinced no inclination to attack them either in front or on the strategic flank, feints only were made in various directions. No single advantage had been secured, the initiative had been surrendered, and the morale of the Imperial troops had been seriously impaired.

Within the course of the next few days Count Gyulai learnt that two additional corps—the 1st (Clam Gallas) and the 2nd (Weigl) were being sent into Italy, and on May 17 he was informed that the Emperor Franz Josef himself would probably shortly assume command of the troops of the Second Army.

On May 14 Urban sent forward a brigade under Colonel Wallon by Casteggio towards Voghera; nowhere was the enemy found in any strength, but a few patrols of Italian lancers were seen in the neighbourhood of Voghera. The Austrians heard here, however, of the arrival in Alessandria of the Emperor Napoleon (he had actually joined his army that very morning), and from information locally obtained and transmitted to the Austrian Headquarters, Gyulai seems to have now formed the conclusion, on what, in the light of subsequent events, seems wholly insufficient basis, that the Allies had the intention either of attempting a crossing at Valenza or Frassinetto, or of advancing by Voghera and Stradella.

To meet such dispositions Gyulai drew up the following scheme, *viz*: should the enemy cross at Valenza he proposed to engage him in front with the 8th, 5th and 2nd Corps, while the 3rd, with one division of the 7th, was to take him in flank by Sartirana and Semiana, the other division of the 7th, covering the flank at Vercelli and Palestro. In the event of the Allies attempting to effect the main crossing at Frassinetto, the 3rd Corps was to hold them in front as long as possible, while the 7th attacked them in flank from Robbio and the 8th from Sartirana—the 3rd Corps being supported by the 5th, and the 7th by the 2nd Corps. Again, should the enemy advance by Voghera on Stradella, the 8th was to fall back fighting—first to the line of the Agogna, then to the Terdoppio and finally to Pavia. The 7th Corps was to retire by Nicorvo, Vigevano and Bereguardo, finally forming a reserve between Pavia and Piacenza.

On May 19 Vercelli was definitely abandoned and the railway bridge was destroyed, the army moving more to the left; the 2nd Corps marched to San Giorgio and Cergnago, the 5th to watch the line of the Po from the Agogna to Mezzana Corti, the 7th moved to Mortara with a brigade on the Agogna between Castel d' Agogna and Nicorvo and a strong post on the Palestro-Vercelli road; the 3rd Corps occupied Trumello, and Army Headquarters was at Garlasco. By this date four brigades of the 9th Corps, with Headquarters, had arrived in Piacenza.

Count Stadion, commanding the 5th Corps, had been sent to Vaccarizza in view of carrying out a reconnaissance in force against the enemy's right, and he now furnished the following report: that there were three regiments of French cavalry between Alessandria and Tortona; that 60,000 men were preparing to cross the Po; that French troops had moved on Robbio by the valley of the Trebbia, and that either on the 19th or 20th a crossing would be attempted between Casale and Cervesina, when the troops moving by the Trebbia would fall upon the rear of the Austrians on the south bank of the Po.

Every report that came into Army Headquarters at Garlasco seems to have confirmed the impression that the Allies would shortly attempt the passage of the Sesia and Po, and Gyulai persuaded himself that the endeavour could only be made in one of three directions: the first—which he considered the least probable—from the line of the Sesia, when the attack would fall upon the 7th Corps, supported by the 8th, 2nd, and 3rd; secondly, by Cambio and Valenza, to be opposed by the 8th, supported by the 3rd, 2nd, and 7th; and thirdly, an advance against Stradella, the Po being crossed at Spessa covered by feints on the Sesia and at Valenza, to be met by the 5th Corps, supported by the 3rd, 2nd, and 8th, crossing at Pavia and Bereguardo.

It will be observed that Gyulai does not seem to have considered the possibility of any advance other than against his immediate front or left.

On the 20th the Allies were distributed as follows:—Sardinians: the 4th Division and the Cavalry Division had moved forward towards Vercelli; the 3rd Division crossed the Po at Casale and occupied Caressana, Stroppiana and Pezzana; the 2nd moved to Gazzo and Motta dei Conti on the Sesia; the 1st to Casale, where was now the King's Headquarters; the 5th remained between Frassinetto and Giarole. French; the 15th Corps (Niel) was at San Salvatore and Valenza; the 2nd (MacMahon) was between Sale and Piovera; the Guard at Alessandria; the 3rd Corps (Canrobert) between Castello and Viguzzolo; the 1st Division of the 5th Corps had a regiment each in Voghera, Tortona and Bobbio; the 1st (Baraguey) was at Casei, Castelnuovo and Voghera. Forey's division in Voghera was covered by ten squadrons of the Sardinian Cavalry Brigade under Sonnaz; three squadrons held the line of the Coppa River between Verretto and Casteggio, another was on the high ground to the right at Codevilla, four squadrons at Pizzale and Calcababbio watched the Staffora and the bridge at Oriolo, while the remaining two squadrons were in Voghera, where also five *pelotons* of the 1st Chasseurs d'Afrique had arrived on the 18th.

The Allies therefore were distributed in three groups: between Vercelli and the junction of the Sesia and Po; between Casale and the Tanaro; and between the Staffora, the Po, the Tanaro and the Voghera—Alessandria road. Of this last group, Forey's division and part of D'Autemarre's (of the 5th Corps) were practically in contact with the troops under Stadion, but the Frenchmen were closely supported by the rest of the 1st Corps at Ponte Curone and at Casei.

It being considered by Gyulai that Urban's presence was no longer required at Stradella, since the 9th Corps was now sufficiently closed up to secure the safety of the left flank of the army, he was ordered back to the Po to assist in preparing and holding the bridgehead now nearing completion at Stella. He had reached Barbianello on his way to Vaccarizza when he was directed to return and place himself under the orders of Count Stadion who was about to endeavour to clear up the situation from Voghera westwards.

For this purpose the following troops had been put at Stadion's disposal: the brigades Gaal and Hess and the brigade Bils of Paumgartten's division—all three of Stadion's own corps; the brigades Braum of the 9th Corps and Schaffgotsche of the Reserve Division—these under Urban—and the brigade Boer of the 8th Corps, then at Vaccarizza.

Stadion directed that the advance should be made in three columns: the left column—the two brigades under Urban—marched by the main road from Broni to Casteggio; the centre column—which Count Stadion accompanied—was commanded by Paumgartten, who had with him the brigades Gaal and Bils, and moved by Barbianello on Casatisma; while Hess formed the right column with his brigade and marched by Verrua and Branduzzo on Oriolo.

The troops with Urban were the only ones who knew the country, and accordingly a battalion from Schaffgotsche's brigade was attached to the other two columns, while Urban's deficiencies, thus caused, were made good by giving him two battalions from Boer's brigade, Boer himself moving up to Barbianello in reserve with two battalions of infantry and the reserve artillery.

It will be noticed that while the force allotted to Stadion for an important operation was drawn from four different units— owing to Gyulai's disinclination to make any temporary altera- tion in the general disposition of his forces—the error of mixing up minor units, strange to one another and their commanders, was still further accentuated by the man in immediate command of the whole.

Urban reached San Giulietta without any opposition, beyond that from some armed peasants, and was ordered at 11 a.m. to push on and capture Casteggio, being promised the support of the brigade Gaal should he need it. Casteggio was occupied in like manner, the few Italian *vedettes* being easily dislodged, and Urban then resolved to move on rapidly and seize Mon- tebello, and, if possible, Genestrello, where he was ordered to stand fast while the right and centre columns advanced upon Voghera. While Urban was moving on Montebello, Gaal, who had been directed to support him and who had reached Ca- satisma, left there at 12.30 and marched on Montebello in two columns—one by the main road, the other by the Coppa valley and Verretto; a reserve was left in Casatisma and the brigade Bils remained in Robecco.

About 1.30 p.m. Stadion met Urban in Montebello, which that officer had just occupied, and there decided that, as the enemy seemed nowhere in strength, the day's operations should cease with the further occupation of Genestrello, a tactical posi- tion of no little importance, standing as it did on an outlying spur of the Apennines and commanding the open country up to the Staffora River, The centre and right columns, moving by cross-country roads, had made but indifferent progress and Sta- dion accordingly issued the following orders for security:—

Urban to send back one brigade to Casteggio, which was to be placed in a state of defence; the other brigade to be posted between Genestrello and Torrazza Coste with cavalry advanced on the Voghera road, and to reconnoitre towards Codevilla.

Gaal's brigade to hold the railway bridge just north of Mon- tebello, and also the line of the Coppa with outposts covering

Casteggio—where the reserve was to be placed—and maintain communication with Urban on the left and on the right with Hess in Branduzzo. Bils was to remain in Casatisma.

These arrangements had been made about 2.30 and orders conveyed to Paumgartten and Hess, when heavy gun firing was heard from the direction of Genestrello; the battalion holding the railway bridge north of Montebello was at once directed to advance along the railway to the assistance of the troops engaged at Genestrello, while Paumgartten was ordered to push on Gaal's brigade to Montebello and Bils to Casteggio, the battalion already in Casteggio to advance to Montebello.

What had happened was that the advance guard in occupation of Genestrello had been suddenly attacked, before any steps had been taken to fortify either that village or Montebello in rear.

General Forey had heard at 12.30 in Voghera of Stadion's advance and at once moved out with two guns and two battalions of the 74th (Beuret's brigade), which happened to be ready, leaving orders for the remainder of the division to follow him as quickly as possible. Arrived at the bridge crossing the Fossagazzo, where two battalions of the 84th were already on outpost, Forey placed his guns in position with a battalion of the 84th on either flank, and held the rest of his troops in reserve. On the right of the road the squadrons of Italian cavalry, of the regiments of Novara and Montferrat, were drawn up.

For some little time the French were greatly out-numbered, and were in no little peril, Braum, advancing by the railway, drove the battalion of the 74th out of the farm and hamlet of Cascine Nuova and occupied it, but the 74th, supported by a battalion of Blanchard's brigade which had now come up, returned to the attack and again possessed themselves of the farm which was now strongly held, while Blanchard extended a battalion of the 91st Regiment between the railway and the main road to strengthen the centre.

The whole of Forey's division had now arrived from Voghera, and that general was prepared to take the offensive. With

Beuret to the right of the road and Blanchard on both sides of the railway, Forey threw forward his right, attacked and captured Genestrello, when Schaffgotsche fell back, hotly pressed, on Montebello. Bils was called up; Braum, who had been fiercely struggling for the recapture of Cascine Nuova, was directed to fall back on Montebello where Gaal had taken up a position to cover the retirement of Schaffgotsche's men; while Hess, who with five battalions had been unable to do more than hold his own on the Staffora against one and a half French battalions, was ordered to retire on Casteggio, and there take up a defensive position.

Preparations for holding Montebello had already been made by some of Gaal's troops and a battalion of Bils' brigade, when the men falling back from Genestrello already made their appearance. There was some confusion before a decision was come to as to which troops were to remain in occupation of the village and which to fall back to Casteggio, when the French advance, energetically pressed by Forey, already reached the high ground close to Montebello.

Beuret's brigade, was ordered to attack on the southwest, while Blanchard, moving along the railway, safeguarded the left. Both brigades were soon heavily engaged among the vineyards and terraces; the fighting—much of it at the closest quarters—continued for two hours; the houses of the village were carried one by one, and finally the cemetery, commanding the road to Casteggio, was stormed, carried with the bayonet and cleared of its defenders. It was here that General Beuret fell mortally wounded.

Bils, in position on the right bank of the Coppa, covered the Broni and Stradella road, while Hess, deploying to the right between the road and the railway, guarded the Casatisma road; between these two brigades the Austrian battalions fell back practically unmolested, Urban on Stradella and Paumgartten on Stella.

To both combatants reinforcements were drawing near when the action closed; Bazaine was hurrying up from Ponte Curone with three regiments of infantry and had reached Genestrello, while Fehlmayr's brigade of the 9th Corps had left Broni for Casteggio, but was halted by Stadion at Borgo San Giulietta.

The action had been principally confined to the infantry, but the Italian cavalry was of the greatest service, made repeated charges on the Austrians, and did all possible to check their advance until the French had collected force sufficient to meet it. Artillery could only play a secondary part in such a thickly cultivated and wooded country. Forey—as has been described—placed two guns on the Fossagazzo bridge to support his attack on Genestrello; he afterwards posted two on the high ground to the right, and employed others near Cascine Nuova, from which the high ground about Montebello is to some extent visible.

The Austrians had two guns on a piece of open ground near the church of Montebello, others on a spur of the hill along which runs the road between the village and the post-road. Here they had constructed a slight breastwork to give cover to the men—an excellent position but for the fact that the ground in front was much hidden by trees.

The following are the numbers engaged and the losses sustained:—

ALLIES:

Two six-gun batteries—one only engaged.

Cavalry	1,294
Infantry	6,933
Killed	105 (officers and men)
Wounded	549
Missing	69

AUSTRIANS:

Artillery	68 guns
Cavalry	1,164
Infantry	22,501

The numbers which actually took part in the action were, however, very much less: e.g., the brigade Bils, over 4,000 strong with eight guns, was not engaged at all.

Killed	331 (officers and men)
Wounded	785
Missing	307

In this mismanaged affair Stadion certainly failed to distinguish himself; he made no real use of his reserves and was over cautious; he had, however, a very difficult task, but all that can be said is that if the movement was injudicious, its execution was indifferent. Forey, on the other hand, acted with much decision and boldness; he took the offensive even with inferior numbers, disregarded the chance of his left being driven back, used every available man for advancing his right, and gained the day by his bold, if somewhat hazardous, attack. The result of the reconnaissance, carried out in so dispirited a manner, was to confirm the Austrian commander-in-chief in the false ideas he had formed as to the intentions of the Allies, for even as late as May 23 he telegraphed to Vienna that:

"the main forces of the French were between Alessandria and Voghera, and that preparations were being made to strike the first blow in the direction of Piacenza,"

and this in spite of the fact that news of the operations conducted by Garibaldi in the north had already reached Austrian Headquarters at Garlasco.

On May 17 Garibaldi, who had been accorded the rank of major-general, was at Biella, where he had collected a force of six battalions of volunteers numbering 3,120 men.

On the 20th he was at Gattinara, and, without opposition and almost unnoticed, he crossed the Sesia next day at Romagnano, owing to the fact that the attention of the Austrians had been diverted to the Lower Sesia by the operations which will be described later. Garibaldi left Borgomanero on the 22nd, and marched *via* Arona on Castelletto, arriving on the 24th at Varese, where he proceeded to raise and organize fresh bodies of volunteers.

Garibaldi's movements had, however, not been altogether

unnoticed: the Military Governor of Milan promptly moved out all his available troops towards Varese, and Gyulai now directed Urban to assume the direction of the operations about to be undertaken in North Lombardy, taking with him the brigade Rupprecht of his Reserve Division. Urban, moving rapidly, reached Camerlata on the 24th, and lost no time in assuming the offensive against the invader.

On the night of the 26th he marched upon and attempted to surprise Varese, but news of his movements had leaked out, and Garibaldi was ready to receive him. The attack was unsuccessful, and Urban fell back upon Rebbio, being followed up all the way and losing considerably. Here he learnt that his other brigade (Schaffgotsche) was being sent to him together with the brigade Augustin of the 9th Corps. Hardly had portions of these reinforcements joined him, when he was again heavily attacked, and was eventually forced to retire on Monza.

On the 29th, however, he moved forward on Varese with all three brigades and was able to occupy that town. Garibaldi having withdrawn his forces in order to attempt the capture of the small fort at Laveno on the Lake Maggiore. Laveno held out, and Garibaldi, returning towards Varese, found Urban in possession, and that his own position had become very critical, hemmed in as he was in the angle between the Ticino, Lake Maggiore and the Swiss frontier, and with his one exit—at Sesto Calende—closed by a force of all arms which Urban had already sent thither.

On June 3, however, Urban hurriedly fell back upon Gallarate, leaving Garibaldi and his Free Corps to reoccupy Varese, where for the present they may be left.

Already on May 18 the Italians had collected pontoons and other materials at Valenza for the re-establishment of communication, which had been interrupted by the partial destruction of the railway bridge. The Austrians, however, opened a cannonade which destroyed several pontoons and caused any proposed attempt at bridging to be abandoned. Vercelli had been evacuated on the 19th by the Austrians, who left only a half brigade of the 7th Corps under Colonel Ceschi, to observe the line of the Sesia in front of Villata and Torrione.

The 4th Italian division (Cialdini) occupied Vercelli, and on the 21st two small columns forded the Sesia—one above and one below the town—and drove back insignificant parties of the Austrians to Orfengo on the Novara road. On the following day Zobel, commanding the 7th Corps, moved the rest of the division to which Ceschi's troops belonged towards Orfengo and Borgo Vercelli, while his other division was concentrating on Robbio. Cialdini with this force in his front and a rising river in his rear judged it best to withdraw, and on the 23rd the Italians accordingly recrossed the river and returned to Vercelli.

King Victor Emmanuel, to support Cialdini's advance, had sent the 1st Division (Castelborgo) towards Candia, the 3rd (Durando) to Caresana, while the 2nd (Fanti) occupied some islands in the Sesia opposite Motta dei Conti, the idea being to facilitate Cialdini's operations by drawing the enemy's attention upon the three other divisions. The 1st Division returned on the 23rd to Casale, and on the night of the 24th-25th Reischach, commanding a division of the Austrian 7th Corps, brought up one of his brigades to support a brigade of Lilia's division at Candia. Here Reischach established during the night a battery of four 12-pounders and four howitzers, opened early in the morning on Fanti's men on the islands, and drove them back to the right bank.

The Emperor of the French had early realized that any attempt to force the passage of the Po and Lower Sesia, where the Austrians were ready to oppose a crossing, would be exceedingly hazardous, if not indeed altogether impossible. On the Austrian left and centre, where the Po could not be passed without a bridge, an advance was evidently awaited. There remained only the Austrian right which had lately been greatly weakened and was covered only by the Sesia, whose upper waters could everywhere be forded by infantry.

For a few days there was no movement of troops on either side; it was the lull before the storm.

In regard to the events above described, Moltke expresses admiration for the rapidity with which Forey collected his division, answered attack with counter-attack, and so snatched victory out of a threatened defeat. Unlike his adversaries he employed the whole strength of his force and won the day.

But it cannot be overlooked that had the Austrians only made proper use of their unquestioned superiority in numbers, Forey must have been defeated. Up to 2 p.m. Schaffgotsche alone was numerically stronger than the French, after which hour the latter may not have had inferior numbers actually on the spot, although Forey had to employ part of his force to hold Hess in check on the left. At Montebello itself the two forces were about equal, but at the time when the Austrians actually commenced their retreat, they possessed at Casteggio a very greatly superior force.

It is said that the Austrians from all time have been partial to such so-called reconnaissances, but undertakings of this description are only of value when it is intended that they should lead to a battle for which every preparation has been made. If the results of a reconnaissance are unfavourable, the operation cannot be quickly enough broken off, whereas if they disclose favourable conditions the opportunity must be seized at once, since they may alter within a very few hours.

Stadion was bound to retire, no matter what immediate advantage he gained, since three French corps were within a few hours' march of Voghera; the Austrian Army, on the other hand, was on the further side of the Po, with no nearer communication between the two banks than that at Vaccarizza—a matter of three marches. It must be considered how far an undertaking is justifiable which entails heavy casualties without compensating results. It is perhaps not impossible that Stadion's movements were in a measure hampered by some such considerations.

What indeed had he gained? He had gleaned no reliable information as to the real strength of the enemy, since he was opposed by only one division, while he could not be certain that even the force with which he had been actually in contact would remain on the spot, since he himself fell back on the next day behind the Po. All he knew for certain was that on May 20 a considerable portion of the French Army was on the Alessandria-Piacenza road in the neighbourhood of Voghera; as much might have been learnt by an officer's patrol intelligently handled.

Chapter 4

The Flank March by the Allies

The Emperor of the French having completed—practically unhindered—the concentration of his troops at Alessandria, now commenced the carrying out of a flank march from right to left under cover of the Po and of the Sesia, so turning the Austrian right on the Novara-Milan road. While all students of the military art are probably agreed that this movement was well designed and admirably executed, the reasons by which it was determined have been greatly criticized.

According to the French *Official History of the War in Italy*, the scheme, if successful, promised great results; Milan must thereby fall into the hands of the Allies, and if Gyulai should attempt to effect a crossing of the Ticino at Bereguardo and Vigevano, the French and Sardinians, in possession of the left bank, should be able to fall in full strength upon isolated Austrian corps which might endeavour to pass over the river. If the Austrians should cross at Pavia, in order to retire upon Belgiojoso and Pizzighettone, they would have to make a serious flank movement across the front of the Allies, who should be able to cut them in two and drive them into the Po.

If they, however, retired on the right bank of the Po by Pavia and La Stella, the Allies—crossing the Adda at Lodi—could seize the passages and drive the Austrians into the Duchies. Finally, if having crossed the Ticino, the Austrians should there offer battle, all that they would gain from a victory would be the recovery of their menaced communications, while a defeat would revive for them at Pavia and Piacenza the disaster of Ulm.

Moltke has the following remarks:

> Any operations by the right bank of the Po required that an army 200,000 strong should advance practically by a single road between the river and the mountains, since that by Bobbio, through the Trebbia valley, could not be of much assistance. Between Alessandria and Piacenza, the road offers a succession of strong positions, and to occupy these in defence the Austrians, already concentrated towards their left, could at any moment debouch by the bridge at Vaccarizza. Finally Piacenza itself must present many difficulties to further onward movement.
>
> The attack of the Allies might have been directed from Valenza and Casale against the front; an advance here, however, led over a country made difficult by a network of rice fields straight at the Austrian entrenched positions. The enemy could in one day mass their main force behind the Agogna, while, if the worst came to the worst, and the Austrians found themselves driven from their positions back to the left bank of the Ticino, they could there again take up a defensive position.
>
> There remained then a third possibility—to turn the Austrian right. For this the railway came to the help of the French, while at Vercelli and Novara they would meet no more than the extreme right of the hostile force. So far, all was plain sailing; it was later that the difficulties began. Communication with Genoa must then be given up, that with Turin must become seriously endangered. The Allies would have their backs to Switzerland—a neutral country. The one indispensable condition for the success of the movement was that the Allies should win all their battles—that consequently tactics must take the place of strategy.
>
> Napoleon, however, could trust his army and he was numerically superior to the Austrians, He acted quickly, suddenly and with energy, and the advantage is generally with

those who thus act, and not with those who merely stand and wait.

Rüstow finds it difficult to decide why Napoleon made up his mind to a line of advance which, if unsuccessful, promised disaster, and which, if all turned out well, offered the most meagre results. He comes to the conclusion that by advancing by Vercelli—Novara—Milan, the Emperor hoped to gain the latter city without bloodshed, believing that Gyulai would fall back over the Ticino without fighting so soon as he saw that his flank was turned. The other reason put forward by Rüstow for Napoleon's action is a political and—it must be confessed—an ungenerous and somewhat sordid one.

He points out that on this flank the troops under Garibaldi—men gathered from all parts of Italy and for the most part red-hot republicans—had pressed forward almost to within sight of the capital of Lombardy, and he suggests that Napoleon and Victor Emmanuel deliberately selected the advance by the left in order by their own presence to minimise the effect of Garibaldi's operations.

Hamley considers that the Allies incurred grave risks by the movement on Novara.

> Had they moved from the Sesia on Mortara and Lomello, and thence on Vigevano and Pavia, they would have perfectly covered both lines to Turin by Casale and Vercelli; and the restoration of the bridge of Valenza behind them would have given the means of passing the Po, and would have materially strengthened their line of operation. Such an operation, in accordance with the circumstances of the case, would have given the army firm grounds from which to manoeuvre for the passage of the Ticino, with better chances of obtaining a decisive strategical success, and with none of the risk of fatal disaster incurred by the flank march.

The whole of this interesting question is discussed at considerable length in *Great Campaigns*, and the author of that book lays stress on two points which no doubt weighed greatly in the decision come to by the Emperor Napoleon: (1) that the difficulty and danger of the flank march were not so great as have been estimated, and that they were virtually reduced to the thirty miles of road which intervene between Casale and Novara, (2) that the nervous anxiety already displayed by the Austrian commander for the safety of his communications doubtless added vigour and boldness to the offensive operations of his adversary It is pointed out that the Austrian left rested on the strong fortress of Piacenza, and that any attempt to turn this flank and the line of the Ticino would have entailed bridging the Po between that stronghold and Pavia at a point or points narrowly watched and strongly guarded.

Again, to force the passage of the Lower Sesia or of the Po, between the Sesia and the Ticino, by attacking the Austrian centre, might have led to exposing the French in detail to the attack of the four Austrian corps, whose concentration could easily and quickly have been effected opposite any threatened crossing point. There remained the third course—the flank march to turn the enemy's right; this offered the prospect of an unopposed passage of the upper Ticino, which—owing to the extravagant ideas of the danger of the flank march held by the Austrian Staff—had been left practically undefended. The author of *Great Campaigns* writes:

> The problem had all along been how to invade Lombardy with the least possible risk. Of the three doors by which such an invasion could be attempted, two were closed, and one, which led circuitously into Lombardy, but direct upon the capital, was alone open. Doubtless to enter by this placed the French Army relatively in a worse strategic position, inasmuch as, if victorious, the enemy would be defeated, not ruined; while if they themselves were repulsed, they would be in a position of grave danger.
> The question, however, arises—what had been gained with reference either to tactical or strategic advantage? It may be answered thus: that the enemy's preparations and

plans had been thwarted. He was called upon to act without being able to deliberate. A battle, if fought, would be engaged under circumstances which enlisted every chance in favour of the French, on the high road to and close to Lombardy, where the attitude of the people was such as to render Gyulai already anxious for his communications.

There has further been much discussion as to whether the idea of an advance by the left was a sudden resolve made on finding the Austrians in strength in the south, or whether the Emperor Napoleon and his military advisers had formed this decision from the first. Colonel Saget, who in 1859 was head of the *Bureau Politique* of the French Headquarter Staff, is said to have stated a year later to a Prussian officer in Paris that during the halt in Alessandria, the left flank march was constantly the subject of discussion among the marshals and the officers of the Headquarter Staff.

While General della Rocca too has mentioned in his *Reminiscences*, that soon after arriving in Alessandria, Napoleon III had discussed with Victor Emmanuel his plans for moving by the left, in the presence of Marshal Vaillant and of della Rocca himself.

On May 26 the Emperor of the French, accompanied by Marshal Vaillant, Generals Frossard and La Marmora, visited Vercelli and at once issued orders for the execution of the great turning movement upon which he had decided.

The Italian Army, holding the left of the position, was directed to mask the flank march of the French columns by attacking the right of the Austrians—formed by Lilia's division of the 7th Corps—and throwing it back upon Robbio. The 3rd French Corps (Canrobert) was directed to support this advance and for this purpose was moved by rail and march route to Casale, where it was concentrated by the 29th.

On the 28th all the other units of the French Army began to conform to the general movement northwards, D'Autemaire's division only, of the 5th Corps, remaining until the 30th, in the vicinity of Voghera with cavalry on the Stradella road, so as to conceal all trace of withdrawal. Frossard had begun on the 27th the construction of trestle bridges over the Sesia at Vercelli, above and below the railway bridge of which the two centre arches had been destroyed by the Austrians; while the Italians commenced the building of a third bridge still higher up the river. Next day Cialdini's division crossed over and occupied some works forming a bridgehead. On the 29th the Italians were concentrated in Vercelli, the 3rd and 4th French Corps and the Guard were at Casale, the 2nd Corps was at Valenza, the 1st at Sale and Bassignana, while the Emperor's Headquarters was at Alessandria.

On the 30th three more Italian divisions commenced the passage of the Sesia, while Canrobert was ordered to cross at Prarolo as soon as the Austrians should have been driven from Palestro. The 4th Division (Cialdini) was to march upon and capture Palestro and there strongly establish itself; the 3rd (Durando) was to seize Vinzaglio; the 2nd (Fanti) having captured Casalino and Confienza was to turn then upon Vinzaglio and hold that village, while Durando moved thence to support Cialdini at Palestro. The 1st Division following the 2nd, was to form a reserve in Casalino, while Cucchiari remained with the 5th Division in Casale.

The four villages thus menaced were held by detachments of the brigades Weigl and Dondorf—having their headquarters at Robbio and Mortara respectively—of Lilia's division, whose nearest supports were the 2nd Corps at Castel d' Agogna and Reischach's brigades of the 7th Corps at Cozzo and Candia.

It was the anniversary of the battle of Goito—the one Italian success in the disastrous campaign of 1848.

Palestro was occupied by three companies, two guns and one troop of Hussars, while in Vinzaglio and Confienza there was only half a company of infantry for the garrison of each village, but all these could be reinforced within an hour from Robbio by ten companies from Weigl's brigade, fourteen of Dondorf's and by fourteen guns; the numbers given as holding the villages do not, of course, include the patrols and outlying picquets which would fall back upon them. Palestro, the most important of the group, stands on the road from Vercelli to Robbio at a point where the Sesia, which here flows close by the road, makes a sharp bend to the east; the village itself stood on a height commanding the plain which was covered with rice-fields and cut up by deep, broad irrigation channels and crossed only by the main road and by the tracks which assisted communication between the villages.

Some 1,600 yards from Palestro was a bridge on the stream called the Roggia Gamara, in front of which the road had been cut in several places. This bridge was held by a small Austrian picquet, which, however, on the advance of the Italians quickly fell back to the high ground in rear. Cialdini now prepared for the attack on the plateau upon which Palestro stood, placed four guns on the road and advanced with the Regina brigade in the first line and the Savona brigade in the second.

The 7th Bersaglieri and the two battalions of the 9th Regiment, well led, succeeded in establishing themselves on the edge of the plateau, but could get no further owing to the heavy musketry and gun fire from the defenders of the village. Lilia had heard about 12.30 of the advance of the Italians, and at once dispatched reinforcements to all the villages threatened. Weigl himself proceeded to Palestro, but on arrival found that the village had been carried and that the Austrians had rallied at the Roggia Borghesa, the edge of which they were holding.

Weigl now attempted to carry forward his reinforcements to the recapture of the village and did indeed succeed in establishing himself temporarily among some of the houses at the eastern outlet. Cialdini, however, was able with his superior numbers to attack energetically again, both from the south and from the Vinzaglio direction, and Weigl was forced to retreat—covered by part of Dondorf's brigade—upon Robbio which he reached about 5 p.m.

While Cialdini was moving upon Palestro, the 3rd Division (Durando), reinforced by two regiments of cavalry, had marched towards Vinzaglio, the position of which is very similar to that of

Palestro. Durando for some reason delayed his attack until midday, by which time reinforcements of five companies of infantry and two guns had reached Vinzaglio *via* Confienza.

Here again the superior strength of the Italians prevailed; the village was attacked on three sides and the Austrians managed to draw off in good order. Part reached Confienza in safety, the remainder with the two guns sought to retire by the Vinzaglio-Palestro road, but were heavily fallen upon by the Italians, then in possession of Palestro, and were driven in great disorder across the rice fields upon Confienza, being obliged to abandon their guns in the heavy ground.

Fanti achieved his object—the occupation of Confienza—without fighting; his movements were slow, and he was further delayed near Borgo Vercelli by an encounter between his advanced troops and a squadron of Austrian cavalry, which had left Novara early that morning to feel for the enemy. Fanti had consequently reached no further than Casalino while fighting was in progress at Palestro and Vinzaglio, and was not able to be of any assistance, but his advance probably hastened the retirement of the troops holding Confienza.

Castelborgo's division reached the vicinity of Confienza late in the afternoon, and the King slept that night at Torrione.

While the Italians had been fighting, the French Army was safely prosecuting the preliminary operations for the flank movement on Novara. Canrobert's three divisions were concentrated at Prarolo by 2 p.m., on the 30th, and as soon as he knew of the success of the Italians, Canrobert commenced the construction of a bridge over the Sesia. The operation was covered on the left bank by the 3rd Zouaves, who belonged to the 5th Corps (Prince Napoleon) and had been sent to Canrobert, but were to act next day under the orders of King Victor Emmanuel. (For this purpose the *zouaves* bivouacked that night at Torrione.)

The Italians strengthened themselves in the villages they had occupied and prepared for an advance next day upon Robbio.

The Austrian Army Headquarters at Garlasco had been kept acquainted with all that had taken place, and Gyulai—though still convinced that the attack was a mere feint to draw his forces northwards—decided to strengthen his right, and towards evening ordered the two divisions of the 2nd Corps to move to Mortara from Cergnago and San Giorgio. Late that night the commander-in-chief himself rode over to Mortara in order to confer with Zobel.

He found that the staff of the 7th Corps was still quite in the dark as to the numbers by which the Austrians had that day been opposed and as to the designs of the enemy. In order then to clear up this dangerous uncertainty, Zobel was ordered to attack early next morning with the division Lilia of his own corps and the division Jellacic of the 2nd; but it was carefully impressed upon him that a reconnaissance in force was all that was required of him.

As a consequence of these orders Count Gyulai was now about to send two divisions against the allied army, which in and about the immediate neighbourhood of Vercelli numbered fourteen divisions of infantry and seven brigades of cavalry; while on the right banks of the Po and Lower Sesia there now stood only four French divisions against which Gyulai had still massed ten divisions of infantry and one of cavalry.

During the night of the 30th, Zobel had conferred with Lilia at Robbio, and it had been decided that the force should advance next morning in three columns; the centre column (the brigades Dondorf and Koudelka) to move by the direct road from Robbio to the east of Palestro, and the left (Szabo) by the Castel d'Agogna-Rosasco road against the south of the village; these two columns, numbering thirteen battalions with one rocket and three field batteries, were thus to attack Palestro in front and flank. The right column under Weigl, and composed of only two battalions and four guns with a troop of cavalry, was to operate against Confienza, and if there successful, to move thence on Vinzaglio. The greater part of the remainder of Weigl's brigade was held back in Robbio in reserve.

The attacks were intended to be delivered simultaneously; Weigl was, however, apparently allowed rather too much time for his longer march and was the first engaged, but by ten o'clock all three Austrian columns had come in touch with the Italian outposts before the intended advance of the enemy upon Robbio had begun. The picquets in front of Palestro were at once driven in and the Austrians established themselves along the line of the Roggia Borghesa, where, however, they were much exposed to and suffered considerably from the fire of the Italians on the plateau.

Here for some time success inclined now to one side, now to the other, until Zobel sent Koudelka's brigade in on the right, when the determined advance of these fresh troops drove back the Italians, while Szabo, pressing on from the south, threatened to establish himself in the outlying houses of the village. The Italian right was now in imminent danger of being thrown back, while Szabo's guns had opened a violent cannonade upon the bridge near Prarolo, where Canrobert was then passing his divisions over the Sesia. Afraid now of being driven from his position, Cialdini sent an urgent appeal for assistance to the 3rd Corps and to the 3rd Zouaves. (This last-named corps had early that morning, taken up a position on Cialdini's extreme right, to the south of Palestro, and along the road leading from that village to Prarolo.)

Zobel, however, was not inclined to press whatever advantage he had gained; it was clear to him that the enemy was present in overpowering strength; the Italians were very strongly entrenched in the village, Szabo's artillery was no match for the guns which Bourbaki had now brought into action against him, and at this moment a report was received from Weigl, that he had been unable to carry Confienza. Zobel therefore directed that the fight be broken off and that the two flank columns should retire respectively upon Rosasco and Robbio; about 1 p.m. the main column withdrew but little molested by the enemy.

Weigl on the right had been given a task impossible of attainment; at or in rear of Confienza were two Italian divisions, the 2nd and 1st, and Fanti, who had made all his preparations for an advance on Robbio, received timely notice of Weigl's approach, so that when this small column—barely a thousand strong—drew near, it found itself opposed to a force of close upon 20,000 men with a numerous artillery, and was unable to advance beyond the Busca.

By this time too Canrobert had passed two of his divisions across the Sesia, and Renault had dispatched four battalions to support Cialdini's left, while Trochu had sent his 1st Brigade to assist the 3rd Zouaves. The whole of the Imperial Guard was now in Vercelli, as was also the 2nd Corps, while the 5th had left Borgo Vercelli, and was marching in the direction of Novara.

Against such a superior force success was hopeless, and Weigl was lucky to be able to effect his retirement on Robbio as easily as he did.

The 3rd Zouaves, finding themselves under fire, had deployed four companies, and these advancing on Cialdini's request for help, soon found themselves in contact with the skirmishers of the 7th Austrian Jägers, who had crossed a canal, only passable at a narrow bridge called the Ponte della Brida, and were at some distance in front of it. Four guns had followed them over and four more had come into action on the banks of the Sesia close by. The left of the *Jägers* was covered by a stream called the Sesietta; this the Zouaves unexpectedly forded and, climbing the bank, drove in the skirmishers and fell with the bayonet upon the flank of the *Jägers*.

These attempted to fall back upon a battalion in rear, but Bourbaki's guns had been firing into this corps during its advance and had thrown it into disorder; the *zouaves* were not to be checked and burst in upon the guns, capturing five. The shattered remnants of Szabo's brigade retreated upon the narrow bridge over the canal; but the *zouaves*, now joined by two Italian battalions, reached it simultaneously, and here wrought terrible havoc, numbers of Austrians being bayoneted or drowned in the canal. Two more guns were here captured by the Italians.

Szabo collected his brigade about 2 p.m. in Rosasco, but in justice to this corps it should be mentioned that it largely consisted—as did many of the other units of the Austrian army—of young soldiers, many of whom hardly knew how to handle their arms, and that the regiments were filled with men recruited in Italy.

On this day the Austrians lost 2,118 in killed, wounded and missing, and the Allies, 601, of which number the casualties in the 3rd Zouaves amounted to 46 killed and 233 wounded.

While the action was still in progress, Gyulai had ordered the commanders of the 2nd and 3rd Corps each to send a division to Robbio to serve both as a support to the troops falling back before the French, and as the nucleus of a fresh force which was to attack the Allies early next day and endeavour to drive them back on Vercelli. These orders were changed in so far as they referred to the 3rd Corps, of which one division (Martini) marched to Mortara, the other (Schönberger) to Castel d'Agogna. Liechtenstein had reached San Angelo with the division detailed from the 2nd Corps, when he met fugitives of Szabo's brigade and learnt through Zobel that the action had ceased. He accordingly arranged to relieve Reischach's division, which had extended to its right up to Celpenchio and San Paolo Leria, and generally to cover the left of the division Lilia of the 7th Corps in Robbio.

Gyulai does not appear to have even yet grasped the fact that the whole of the allied forces were gathering on his right flank, for he issued instructions for the 8th Corps to hold Breme and Sartirana in greater strength, the 5th Corps was directed to occupy Ottobiano and Ferrara each with a brigade, and all troops in that neighbourhood were ordered to be on their guard against any attempt to cross the river at Candia and Frassinetto.

On the evening of the 31st Gyulai telegraphed to Vienna that he had cancelled the orders for attack next day, as the enemy appeared to be in overwhelming force.

Of the reinforcements recently ordered from Austria to Italy, the 1st Corps (Count Clam) was directed on Magenta—one brigade to Monza—the 10th to Adria, Monselice and Nogara, while the 11th was ordered to proceed to Borgoforte.

On this night the Allies were thus disposed: their front line ran from Cameriano to Palestro; on the left, the 4th Corps at Cameriano lay *à cheval* the Vercelli-Novara road. In the centre stood three Italian divisions, while on the right was the 3rd French Corps and the 4th Italian division. The 2nd Corps was at Borgo Vercelli, the Imperial Guard in Vercelli, the 1st Corps was at Casale, D'Autemarre's division of the 5th Corps was partly at Tortona, partly in Alessandria, while the 5th Italian division occupied Casale, Valenza and Alessandria.

It had been originally intended that the Italians should move on Robbio at daybreak on June 1, drive out the Austrians and pursue them to this side of Nicorvo, so as to gain possession of the bridge over the Agogna, while King Victor Emmanuel, retaining a substantial part of his force at Robbio, should there occupy a good position whence to command the roads leading to Rosasco and San Angelo. Canrobert was to occupy Palestro with two divisions, and Confienza, Vespolate and Borgo Lavezzaro with the other. The 4th Corps (Niel) was to move direct on Novara; in fact, the move on Robbio was intended merely to mask the march of the main strength of the army on Novara.

The result of the action at Palestro—which ensured the success of the flank movement—had necessitated some alterations in these arrangements, and it was now considered that the move on Novara was sufficiently covered by the forces under the King and Marshal Canrobert, and that everything showed that the Austrian centre was at Mortara and that the attention of the enemy was still fixed upon the Po and the Lower Sesia.

The Novara road therefore was practically open. Since Novara would henceforth be the new base for the army, it was of the utmost importance to cover Vercelli and the Sesia bridges, and General Frossard at once commenced the construction of a bridgehead on the left bank at Vercelli.

Novara was held only by two battalions of infantry and two guns, and these, attacked at daybreak by Failly's division of the 4th Corps, fell back on the bridge at San Martino. Niel passed through the town and drew forward his whole corps upon the Mortara road; the 3rd Division (Failly) was placed at Olengo, the

2nd (Vinoy) to the right of the Mortara road at La Biccoca, and the 1st (De Luzy) at Torrione Quartara with the right resting on the Agogna. The 2nd Corps encamped between the 4th and Novara, and Desvaux's cavalry division reconnoitred to Vespolate, Trecate and Galliate without seeing anything of the enemy.

The French Headquarter Staff could now no longer hope that so extended a movement had altogether escaped notice and fully expected that an attack would be made upon the Allies by the Austrians, but against this the former were now well prepared.

If Gyulai attacked towards Vercelli, the Italians, the 1st and 3rd Corps were strongly posted to meet him—with the right on the Sesia and the left covered by the difficult ground about the Agogna—while the troops at Novara could seriously menace the flank of any such attack. If, on the other hand, Gyulai attacked on the line Mortara—Novara the advantage to the Allies would be at least equally great; the blow could only be delivered on a narrow front, easy to defend and with both flanks covered by rivers; La Biccoca and Olengo were strongly held, and the troops at Vercelli could menace the line of the Austrian retreat on Mortara while keeping open that of the Allies by Vercelli.

The first report of the advance upon Novara was in Gyulai's hands at 8.30 a.m. and by 10 o'clock the following orders had been issued: the 2nd Corps to march to Mortara and go into bivouac on the east of the town; Lilia's division of the 7th Corps at Robbio to fall back on Castel d'Agogna and there form a reserve for Reischach's division of the same corps which was west of San Angelo; Schönberger's division of the 3rd Corps, hitherto at Castel d'Agogna, to move at once on Robbio and take over the duties of Lilia's division; Martini's division of the 3rd Corps to send a brigade each to Albonese and Nicorvo; while finally, Mensdorff's cavalry division was to concentrate in Borgo Lavezzaro, to patrol towards Nibbiola and Garbagna and keep touch with the 3rd Corps.

Little more than an hour later fresh orders were issued to Schwartzenberg, who was now directed to send Martini's division to Vespolate to hold the enemy in check, supporting it with that of Schönberger to the north of Mortara. By the night of June 1, therefore, Gyulai had drawn at least some of his divisions northwards to meet the enemy about Novara, whose strength he now estimated at from 50,000 to 60,000 men; his troops in this quarter now faced west and north, his outpost line being here drawn along the Agogna to Nibbiola, then at right angles across the main road to the Terdoppio, then to Cassalnovo and from here to the Ticino.

To the south Stadion (8th Corps) was directed to draw in as much as possible to Lomello, employing chiefly mounted troops on his outpost line, and all corps commanders were warned of the probability of an early and general retirement behind the Ticino,

Meanwhile the small force driven from Novara had fallen back upon and occupied the bridgehead at San Martino, whence the commander was calling for reinforcements. These were to be furnished by Count Clam with the still incomplete 1st Corps which was hurrying up by forced marches from Milan; and at 2 a.m. on the morning of the 2nd Clam had occupied Magenta and thrown a brigade into San Martino.

It would seem then that Gyulai had now begun to hope that Clam and Urban between them might be able to hold back the left of the Allies until the Austrian Commander should be able to pass his corps over the Ticino and mass them about Magenta for the defence of the capital of Lombardy.

In discussing the attack by the Austrians in the second day's fighting about Palestro, Moltke has much to say of the ignorance of the Austrians in regard to the forces by which they were likely to be opposed. He admits that possibly the nature of the country prevented the Austrians from recognising that they had in their front the whole Italian Army, but the action of the 30th should have at least made them realise that very considerable forces were already on the left bank of the Sesia.

They can hardly have supposed that the Italians would have thus cut themselves off from their base and exposed themselves isolated to certain defeat, while their allies were marching on Piacenza. Being where they were, the Italians must be supported by the French, and after the events of the 30th at latest, the Austrians should, Moltke considers, have had no more anxiety whatever about their southern flank. The French must now either cross at Valenza and Casale or follow the Italians—the latter being the more likely procedure.

Leaving then two divisions at Robbio and one at Cozzo, the whole of the remainder of the Austrian Army—even including the 9th Corps—might in one march have been concentrated between Mortara and Garlasco. If the French crossed in their front, the two Robbio divisions should have been able to hold the Italians, while 90,000 Austrians fell upon the French engaged in the passage of the river. If, on the other hand, the French followed the Italians, it was certain that they would not attempt to cross the Ticino without either attacking the Austrians or being themselves attacked.

Before anything it was, however, vital that the Austrians should concentrate.

Speaking of Napoleon's resolve to push part of his army at once on to Novara after the second action at Palestro, Moltke points out that, however sound these dispositions may have appeared to the French, there was the danger of being forced back into the mountains in the event of a check at Novara; that Novara and Palestro were half a day's march apart, that the initiative lay with the opponent, and that had demonstrations been made at the same time upon each portion of the divided French forces, it would not have been easy to recognise which was the real attack.

Moltke, however, sees in the position of the Allies just one of those dangers which every army must occasionally face when a great stake is being played for; one of those crises which cannot be avoided, and which history, after the event, describes as either a bold undertaking or an error in strategy.

Since, however, neither portion of the divided army was likely to be greatly inferior in strength to whatever might be brought against them, Napoleon could well afford to leave something to chance without risking too much.

CHAPTER 5

The Austrians Recross the Ticino

"There are two passages over the Ticino in the neighbour-hood of Novara—that of Buffalora and that of Turbigo. The first is the principal one and over it runs the main road from Novara to Milan. A magnificent bridge of large granite blocks, constructed in 1810 by the French, connects the two banks of the river. The other passage at Turbigo is from five to six miles up the river and serves as an auxiliary means of communica-tion between the two sides of the Ticino. Although tolerably frequented in the time of the Austrians, and provided with the inevitable passport and custom-house offices, it could only boast of a ferryboat; the intention being to discourage as much as possible the intercourse between Sardinia and Lombardy and restrict it to a few main arteries of communication. It was be-tween these two passages that the Allies had to choose, for they were the only points on the river in the neighbourhood of their position to which regular roads led, and were consequently the only ones accessible to a large army.

"The Ticino, like most of the feeders of the Po, is skirted on both sides by a plateau which, according to the capricious wind-ings of the stream, approaches and recedes, leaving sometimes only a narrow space between it and the river, and at other places a distance of a couple of miles. This plateau evidently indicates the old bed of the river, through which the waters have gradu-ally eaten their way. Both at Ponte di Buffalora and Ponte di Turbigo the river approaches close to the plateau on the right bank. Owing to the action of the stream this latter has been worn away and shows a bold, precipitous line towards the river which runs forty to seventy feet below it. On the left bank, on the contrary, the plateau is at some distance from the river, leaving a space of more than a mile, which, by means of irrigation, has been converted into a rich plain covered with crops and trees. The right bank consequently completely commands the left, which is therefore not defensible.

"The Austrians, well aware of this circumstance and yet anxious to have a *point d'appui* in case of need, constructed a *tête de pont* on the right bank at San Martino on the road to the Ponte di Buffalora. Coming from Novara this road passes through a well-cultivated district abounding in crops of every kind, especially Indian corn, and studded with mulberry and willow trees. This lasts as far as the village of Trecate, which is just half-way from Novara to the Ticino. Soon after leaving Trecate the aspect of the country changes; the signs of cultivation disappear, and an open, heathy country, with here and there a solitary tree, follows, through which the road runs in an almost straight line to the plateau overhanging the Ticino.

"Just at the edge of the plateau, overlooking the river and commanding a magnificent view over the opposite bank, is a cluster of houses. This is San Martino, so called from an old inn of the same name. Besides this inn there were buildings which served formerly as the Sardinian custom-house and police office, to which in later years the railway station had been added; here was formerly the limit of the Sardinian territory and the seat of the frontier authorities. Beyond San Martino the road descends abruptly towards the bridge which is scarcely two hundred yards distant from it.

"This then was the point chosen by the Austrians for a *tête de pont*. Evidently they attached great importance to the position, for no labour had been spared to convert the approach to the Ticino into a formidable looking entrenchment. Not only were the cluster of houses and the railway station included, but likewise a solitary house a quarter of a mile further north. The whole space thus closed in comprised an area of at least half a square mile, and all this ground was converted into a large work, carried back on both flanks to the very edge of the plateau, and provided with a wide ditch, parapets, and embrasures for seventeen guns.

"While so much care had been taken to guard the approaches to the Ponte di Buffalora, nothing was done by the Austrians to defend the passage at Turbigo, except removing the ferry-boat which served as the means of communication at that place. This circumstance alone would have been sufficient to point out the passage of Turbigo as the one to be preferred; not that the *tête de pont* at San Martino was very formidable—it looked more so than it was in reality—but however weak, it was sufficient to allow a few thousand determined men to defend themselves for some time, even against superior forces, and thus gain time for the Austrian Army to come up and occupy a position behind the Ticino on the road to Milan.

"Besides this obvious reason for effecting a passage at Ponte di Turbigo rather than at Ponte di Buffalora, there were two even more cogent grounds for this choice. The first of these was that Ponte di Turbigo is six miles higher up the river and was consequently not much further removed from the main body of the Austrians, which had to come up from Mortara and Vigevano; thus there was more chance of gaining the opposite bank before any large body of Austrian troops could be brought to oppose this passage. The second was that by crossing at Turbigo without delay, it was possible to gain not only the left bank of the river, but likewise the opposite bank of the Naviglio Grande Canal and thus to overcome this formidable obstacle and open the road to Milan. The canal is here only one and a quarter miles from the river and its banks are less steep and precipitous than lower down; the Naviglio Grande issues from the river opposite Oleggio and runs parallel to the Ticino, at a distance varying from half a mile to four miles, until it reaches Abbiategrasso where it takes a sudden turn in the direction of Milan."

On the afternoon of June 2 General Camou received orders to endeavour to effect the passage of the Ticino at Turbigo with the 2nd Infantry Division of the Imperial Guard, while Espinasse, with the 2nd Division of the 2nd Corps, moved on Trecate and San Martino.

Camou reached the river bank at 3.45 p.m. and saw nothing of the enemy beyond a very few scouts, who had occupied a small house on the left bank and who withdrew as soon as the Chasseurs of the Guard commenced to cross in small boats. Camou placed twelve guns on the high ground to the left of the road and twelve more on the river bank; by these the whole of the approaches to the spot where he proposed to throw a bridge—on the site of the old ferry—were thoroughly commanded. Covered by these guns and four companies of *chasseurs*, who were passed over to the left bank by five o'clock, the construction of the bridge was at once commenced under the supervision of General Frossard, who had accompanied Camou.

While the work was in progress the 1st Brigade (Manèque) took up a position on the high ground to right and left of the road and the cavalry reconnoitred towards Villa Fortuna. At 7.30 the bridge was finished, some temporary works had been thrown up for its protection, and so far the only hostile troops which had been seen were some mounted men of the 1st Corps, who quickly fell back.

Manèque now crossed over with his brigade—Decaen taking the positions he vacated—and as the French troops became visible on the left bank a squadron of Austrian cavalry was seen to hurriedly leave Turbigo; it was learnt that these were some of Urban's men from Gallarate, During the night Turbigo itself was occupied—the wooden bridge over the Grand Canal having been found intact—and at daybreak on the 3rd, while Turbigo was being rapidly placed in a state of defence, Camou's troops were thus disposed; two battalions under Manèque in front of Turbigo, two others on the right bank under Decaen, two in the works at the bridge on the Ticino, and two battalions occupying the bridge over the Grand Canal.

The Emperor had thus secured, with unexpected facility, a

crossing place over both the river and the canal; but before preparing to pass over the whole of the allied army it was of the first importance to learn something definite of the movements of the enemy, and Niel was ordered to carry out a reconnaissance in force in the direction of Mortara on the morning of the 3rd. Niel took with him Luzy's entire division and one brigade of that of de Failly, the whole of the remainder of the 4th Corps being held in readiness to follow him if required.

The three brigades left La Biccoca at sunrise in two columns, one marching on Vespolate by the road and railway, the other moving on Terdobbiate and Tornaco by Olengo; arrived at Garbagna it was reported to the right column that the enemy, who had been in strength at Vespolate, had moved on Tornaco; but at Vespolate the French learnt that the town had been evacuated at 3 a.m., and that the enemy had moved off in the direction of Vigevano,

It was at once apparent that the Austrians were massing on the Ticino, but on which bank was as yet uncertain, and to guard against any attempt upon him by the right bank the Emperor decided to keep the 1st, 3rd, and 4th Corps in front of Novara, while with the 2nd and the Imperial Guard he prolonged his line to the left and secured the passages of the Ticino.

MacMahon was consequently directed to concentrate the whole of the 2nd Corps at Turbigo, while Mellinet's division of the Guard was ordered to move on at once upon Trecate and San Martino, relieving Espinasse, who was to rejoin MacMahon.

June 2 was to find the irresolution and vacillation of the Austrian Commander at their worst. During the small hours of the morning he issued orders for the 7th and 2nd Corps to move at once—the former to Olevano (south of Mortara) and the latter to Mortara. Stadion was directed to make every preparation for the retirement of the 5th and 8th Corps behind the Ticino at the shortest possible notice, and a few moments later Gyulai informed Count Clam that he was about to effect his retirement across the river and that the 2nd and 3rd Corps would cross at Vigevano and fall into line on the left of the 1st Corps. He ordered Clam at once to recall Urban from Varese.

The 7th Corps commenced its retirement at 9 a.m., covered by Weigl's brigade, and fell back practically unopposed, part by Nicorvo and the remainder by Castel d'Agogna. The 2nd Corps, moving by Ceretto and Castel d'Agogna, had almost reached Mortara, when its commander received fresh instructions, from which it appeared that the withdrawal over the Ticino had now been cancelled.

At 11.30 the 7th Corps was ordered not to march on Olevano, but to remain at Castel d'Agogna, detaching a brigade to Nicorvo and reoccupying Robbio with a battalion. Zobel, however, who only received this order on the Agogna, considered its execution to be impossible, since he was convinced that Robbio was ere this in the occupation of the enemy; he contented himself there- fore with dropping Weigl's brigade in Ceretto, and occupying San Angelo, Castelnovetto and Celpenchio with detachments of cavalry and infantry.

At this hour Gyulai announced that for the present he should remain on the right bank of the Ticino and that Urban was to pursue his operations against Garibaldi, but at midday Gyulai again changed his mind and telegraphed to the Emperor Franz Josef that he had now ordered the retirement of the army behind the river, and that he hoped by next day to have taken his stand between Magenta and Pavia.

The 2nd Corps was the first to recross the Ticino; it passed the river at Vigevano, and late at night went into bivouac at Soria. The 7th Corps marched to Vigevano from Castel d'Agogna; was greatly delayed near Mortara by its route crossing that of the 2nd Corps; reached its bivouac on the right bank, thoroughly worn out, between 10 p.m. and midnight, and finally marching next morning by Abbiategrasso reached Gaggiano, where it was to be held in reserve.

The 3rd Corps, which was still about Nicorvo, Borgo Lavezzaro, Nibbiola and Vespolate, was informed of the movements of the 2nd and 7th Corps, and was ordered to retire on Vigevano as soon as the 7th Corps had cleared the bridge, and, having crossed over, to move towards Abbiategrasso, taking up a position south of Ozero. The passage of the river at Cassalnovo was to be safeguarded; the bridge and bridgehead at Vigevano were to be held as long as possible, and to be destroyed if evacuation became imperative. The Cavalry Division was to move with the 3rd Corps and march on the 4th from Abbiategrasso to Magenta, to be there placed at the disposal of Count Clam.

Late on the 2nd, Gyulai communicated to Clam his intention of retiring next day, and informed him that he would be reinforced in Magenta on the 3rd day by the 2nd Corps and on the 4th by the Cavalry Division. Clam was directed to send half a brigade, with cavalry, to Castano to watch the crossings at Turbigo and Tornavento; he was ordered to hold the bridgehead at San Martino at all costs, while if the garrison were forced to retreat the guns were to be spiked, the magazine blown up and the bridge destroyed. He was also informed that Army Headquarters would next day be at Rosate and that the 5th Corps would also be there, while the 8th would reach Binasco.

During the night of the lst-2nd the commander of the 1st Corps had been making great efforts to push troops up to San Martino, and by early morning of the latter date the strength of the force holding the bridgehead—all belonging to his 2nd (Cordon's) Division—was five battalions with fourteen guns, five of which were guns of position; there was in addition half a rocket battery; a squadron of cavalry had been sent towards Turbigo, while between Buffalora and Ponte di Magenta, on the left bank of the Grand Canal, was a reserve of two battalions of infantry with a horse-battery.

During the forenoon of the 2nd, Clam himself reached San Martino and went round the defences, of which he formed a very poor opinion. Not only did he consider the works of weak profile, but the construction was faulty; the perimeter was so great that, in his opinion, at least three brigades would be required adequately to man the works—which were, moreover, quite open to attack on either flank—while the crops and undergrowth were so high in the immediate neighbourhood as to permit of hostile approach quite undetected. Clam, however, decided that the place must be held at all costs, and gave orders for such improvements to be carried out as time and means permitted.

The unsatisfactory state of the defences at San Martino was not improved by the unfortunate condition of the men who were to hold them. These had out-marched their supplies and were moreover greatly exhausted by the exertions they had recently undergone. Clam made what arrangements he could, gave orders that requisitions were to be made on the inhabitants, and returned to Magenta.

Towards evening a report reached the Headquarters of the 1st Corps from San Martino that the enemy were establishing some guns in battery on the Trecate road; Clam at once sent his Chief of Staff forward to investigate this report, which on arrival he found to be confirmed; he learnt also at San Martino that requisitions had produced but very few supplies and that the worn-out troops were practically without rations.

Applications for supplies had been made to Abbiategrasso, where there was a depôt; but the local supply officer had reported that his stores were inconsiderable and that for the issue of what little he had he was wholly without transport of any kind. At this time (8 p.m.) a report was forwarded by the officer commanding the squadron which had been sent towards Turbigo, that the Allies had already there thrown a bridge over the river and were that day in occupation of the left bank.

Clam had now at once to make up his mind as to how he should act, for there was no time to acquaint Gyulai with this new development and await his instructions; it seemed to the officer commanding the 1st Corps that by continuing to hold the bridge-head at San Martino he was in danger of exposing his troops at Magenta to an attack in overwhelming force, while the defenders of San Martino were engaged with an enemy advancing from the direction of Trecate; if Cordon's men in San Martino were driven from the defences—of which Clam had already formed so low an opinion—their retreat on Magenta would be no easy one, since the road for a considerable distance was carried along an embankment.

He had no immediate prospect of support, for although he had been informed of the approach of the 2nd Corps, there was no reason to believe that it could reach Magenta before the night of the 3rd. About 10 p.m. therefore Clam gave orders for the bridge works to be evacuated and for the bridge to be blown up at daybreak. The five big guns could not be brought away, so these were spiked; the troops were withdrawn from the entrenchments and drawn up in a defensive position on the left bank.

At dawn the bridge was blown up, but the damage done was inconsiderable; the mines had been laid in the second pier from the left bank so as to bring down the two arches which it supported, but although the two arches were displaced, the top of the pier only gave way, and the bridge, though temporarily impassable for cavalry and artillery, was quite fit for the passage of infantry. Whatever the cause of the failure, the result to the Allies was most important, for they had now two undisputed communications with the left bank.

Clam gave orders that another attempt should at once be made to more thoroughly effect the demolition of the bridge, but the officer commanding the engineers stated that he had no more powder; there was none procurable in Magenta and urgent requisitions were sent for some to Pavia; in the meantime, and in view of a possible forced retirement to the line of the Grand Canal, the engineers were directed to prepare for demolition all the bridges over it between Bernate and Robecco.

Early on the morning of the 3rd, Cordon left for the direction of Turbigo to endeavour to discover in what strength the enemy had crossed. He took with him four complete battalions and portions of two others, a horse battery and part of the rocket battery which had formed a portion of the armament of the defences at San Martino.

Gyulai had issued the following instructions to the two corps composing the left wing of his army:

The 8th Corps to move today (the 2nd) to Trumello, the division of the 5th Corps, now in San Nazzaro to Garlasco; on the 3rd both corps to cross the Ticino at Bereguardo. Sternberg's division of the 5th Corps to march from Mortara *via* Gambolo to Borgo San Siro where orders should reach them.

In accordance with the above, Stadion's divisions bivouacked for the night at Garlasco and Borgo San Siro, while the 8th Corps marched at 4.30 from Lomello through Ottobiano and halted for the night in Trumello.

The decision to cross the Ticino was also communicated to the 9th Corps and the commander was directed to leave some troops between Stradella and Piacenza and to place the remainder of his force between Castelpuste Orlengo and Corte Olona; the Po was to be watched below Vaccarizza, and the 9th Corps was to arrange the safe passage of all sick and wounded down the river in boats to Borgoforte, whence they would be forwarded *via* Mantua to Verona.

At 8 p.m. Gyulai received a telegram stating that Feldzeugmeister Baron Hess was being sent by the Emperor to confer with Gyulai on the spot, that he had started for Milan where he expected to arrive at midnight and where full information regarding the movements and dispositions of the units composing the Second Army was to be sent him. Gyulai at once dispatched a special officer to Milan with the following report (this officer appears, however, to have missed Baron Hess):—

The Army will tomorrow (3rd) be thus disposed:
The 1st and 2nd Corps and the Cavalry Division in Magenta, with one brigade at Castano, to watch the passages of the Ticino at Tornavento and Turbigo.
The 3rd Corps at Abbiategrasso.
The 7th Corps in reserve at Gaggiano.
The 5th Corps between Morimondo and Besate.
The 8th Corps in reserve west of Binasco with one division in Bereguardo.

The 9th Corps between Piacenza and Corte Olona with one brigade in Piacenza and one in the bridge-head at Vaccarizza.

These arrangements permit of a frontal defence of the Ticino in case—which is improbable—the enemy should attempt to cross between Magenta and Bereguardo. He is, however, far more likely to turn our flank by crossing at Turbigo and Tornavento.

About five o'clock on the morning of the 3rd, Hess met Gyulai at Bereguardo and two hours later—in consequence of what Gyulai appears afterwards to have described as more or less of a "mandate"—the 5th and 8th Corps were ordered to stand fast wherever the order to do so should reach them; the 3rd was directed—if its passage of the river was already completed—to take up a position on the left bank with Dürfeld's brigade in Vigevano, but, if it had not already crossed, the whole corps was to remain in Vigevano.

At 9 a.m. Gyulai heard through the 2nd Corps in Soria, that the Allies had already bridged the Ticino at Turbigo and that they were in strength on the left bank; that Clam had decided to withdraw from San Martino and destroy the bridge; and that the 2nd Corps was moving at once on Magenta. An hour later came the disturbing news that the attempt to blow up the bridge had failed, while it was suggested that the 2nd and 7th Corps should march as speedily as possible north- wards towards the San Mar-tino-Milan road.

Orders were then sent to Cordon that he should proceed no further northward until the 2nd Corps should have drawn near-er to Magenta, but a report now came in from him that he had reached and occupied Cuggiono at 7 a.m. and had pushed pa-trols towards Turbigo, Castano and Buscate; he had, however, as yet learnt nothing definite as to the strength of the allied forces at Turbigo. Cuggiono was occupied by one battalion, three guns and half a squadron of cavalry; in Bernate was one battalion and another was in Ponte nuovo di Magenta, but the two battalions which had been sent to Inveruno had moved out, without orders, in the direction of the enemy and Cordon knew nothing of their whereabouts.

About this hour—between 9 and 10 a.m.—Hess finally withdrew his objections to the movements eastwards of the corps still on the right bank of the Ticino, and it was therefore directed that they should be carried out as previously ordered; but the interference with the "man on the spot" had of course entailed a cessation of all movement during not less than six hours.

Clam was informed, but was given strict orders not to push too far to the north as this would weaken the line almost to breaking point; Gyulai expressed his intention of attacking in force the flank of the enemy should his main body cross at Turbigo, but he pressed Clam for detailed information of the strength of the Allies at that point.

At 3 p.m. Gyulai left Rosate with his staff for Magenta, and during the course of the day the retirement of the Second Army behind the Ticino was continued and was accomplished as follows:—

The 3rd Corps began at daybreak to evacuate its positions in front of Mortara; Hartung's brigade moved on Vigevano by Tornaco and thence down the valley of the Terdoppio; Metzlar marched by Cassalnovo, and Ramming direct on Vigevano where Dürfeld's brigade had already arrived. Here, however, the passage of the river could not be proceeded with for several hours. This was caused in some degree, no doubt, by bad staff work, but also by the contradictory orders which had been issued, and by the fact that the difficulties of communication had in some cases delayed the receipt of instructions and in others had prevented their receipt altogether.

The 2nd Corps which had reached and bivouacked at Soria appears to have been strung out between that place and the Ticino; Liechtenstein was preparing to continue his march on Magenta on the morning of the 3rd, when he found that the Cavalry Division, the head of the 7th Corps (Reischach's division), and the baggage of both were closing up to him from the bridge in rear. Liechtenstein then allowed the cavalry to pass through his corps, but directed Reischach to halt and follow the 2nd Corps.

(The cavalry moved straight on Magenta and went in to bivouac behind the town on the high ground.) Of the 2nd Corps, Kintzl's brigade occupied Robecco and Ponte Vecchio each with two battalions, while the others moving on Magenta went into camp, Baltin and Szabo to the right and left of the road respectively and Koudelka in rear of the town.

The bulk of the 7th Corps only cleared the bridge at Vigevano about 11 a.m. and reached Abbiategrasso at two o'clock. Here Lilia halted while Reischach marched on to Cerella and there spent the night. As Abbiategrasso had been allotted to the 3rd Corps, Zobel moved out Lilia's division to Casteletto where it arrived between one and two in the morning of the next day. In consequence of all these delays—under the circumstances not altogether unavoidable—the 3rd Corps was not across the bridge until after 4 p.m. and did not reach Abbiategrasso until long after night had fallen.

The 5th Corps had already reached the bridge at Bereguardo with the head of Sternberg's division, while that of Paumgartten had just left Garlasco, when—about 8 a.m.—the order to stand fast was received. When about 11.20 this was again cancelled, Stadion began passing over his brigades and four of them [1] had crossed the river soon after 3 p.m. Bils was directed to follow after the 8th Corps. Stadion took up the line—Morimondo—Coronate—Binasco—Fallavecchia—Besate for the night.

Benedek with the 8th corps left Trumello at 2 p.m., crossed the bridge at Bereguardo during the early hours of the 4th, and established himself at Bereguardo and Motta Visconti.

The units of the 9th Corps were too scattered to admit of their being collected to cross to the other side of the Po on the 3rd, but all arrangements were made, the outposts were gradually withdrawn, and the corps, with the exception of Fehlmayr's brigade, which remained in Stradella, was concentrated about

---

1. It will have been noticed that the 1st, 5th, 8th, and 9th Corps had each five brigades, the other corps four only.

Piacenza on the 4th.

To complete the tale of the Austrian movements on the 3rd, it only remains to say that on this day Urban withdrew the bulk of his troops from Varese to Gallarate, sending some mounted men further south towards Lonate Pozzolo, whence news of the action which this day took place was conveyed to him.

It is now time to return to the operations of the French.

About 2 p.m. on the 3rd, MacMahon with his 1st Division (La Motterouge) arrived at the bridge at Turbigo, and crossing the river accompanied by General Camou, he mounted the tower of Robecchetto; from here he saw Cordon's advanced troops within a few hundred yards hurrying to seize the village, behind which MacMahon had proposed establishing his corps in bivouac, Robecchetto is rather more than two miles from Turbigo on the road to Buffalora, and, like both villages, is situated on the edge of the plateau skirting the valley of the Ticino; there are two roads from Turbigo to Robecchetto—one leading to the southern, the other to the western portion of the village, while the road to Buffalora leaves the village in an easterly direction. The occupation of Robecchetto was to the French of the first importance—both to cover the bivouac of the 2nd Corps and to ensure the success of any further movement on Buffalora and Magenta.

On his return to Turbigo from the front, MacMahon found that a regiment of Turcos was at the head of the column, and he at once sent them forward to occupy the village or dislodge its defenders. The 1st battalion of Turcos, formed in column of divisions and preceded by two companies of skirmishers, was to attack the village from the south; the 3rd battalion, forming the left column and similarly disposed, was to attack it from the west; while the 2nd, somewhat in rear, was to form a reserve to both. The other regiment, the 45th, of this brigade, and later the 2nd brigade of La Motterouge's division, were sent forward— the 2nd brigade by Castano—in support of the Turcos, who were closely followed by a battery of artillery. Arrived at Robecchetto the French found the Austrians in position at the entrance and were received by a brisk fire, but the Turcos rushing forward without firing, threw themselves on the Austrians with the bayonet. In a few minutes the village was cleared and the Austrians were retreating on Buffalora. In order to check the pursuit Cordon brought up some guns which stopped the Turcos for a moment, but the French artillery replied and the rout was soon complete. Equally unsuccessful was a demonstration made by some of Urban's cavalry on the left, from the direction of Castano; it was met by a battalion of the 65th of the line with two guns and thrown back.

One field gun fell into the hands of the French, whose loss is given in MacMahon's report to the Emperor as eight killed and forty-two wounded; the casualties among the Austrians amounted to twenty-five killed, forty-six wounded and thirty-five missing—the greater part of these losses occurring in the 14th Jäger Battalion.

The 2nd Corps was by this time across the Ticino, and its brigades bivouacked in a semi-circle round the northwest and south of the village of Turbigo with Camou's division in rear.

General von Caemmerer, in his work Magenta, mentions certain facts in connexion with the retirement of the Austrians across the Ticino which I have not found elsewhere. He states that immediately after the actions at Palestro, there was a serious difference of opinion between Gyulai, the commander-in-chief, and Kuhn, his chief of the staff, as to the course to be adopted. Gyulai was in favour of complete retirement behind the Mincio, and for this proposal von Caemmerer has a good deal to say that is not altogether unfavourable.

It is true that by such a retirement the whole of Lombardy was handed over to the invaders, but a similar course of action had been pursued in 1848-49, and had led to final victory and to the abdication of the then King of Sardinia. If the Austrians were inclined thus to postpone the ultimate decision until the whole of their 1st, 10th and 11th Corps had joined the army, they would then have had the preponderance in strength on their side, and a victory would have enabled them to drive back the

Allies to the west, while their forces at Borgoforte and Piacenza could have advanced towards Genoa.

"Here," says von Caemmerer, "was a very practical method of bringing the campaign to a successful conclusion." Had the retreat been arranged on the night of June 1, it could have been carried through without interruption.

Kuhn, on the other hand, urged his chief repeatedly to take the offensive in the direction of Novara, and declares that twice—on the nights of May 30 and June 1—he drafted orders for such an advance. On the latter occasion the attack—to be made by the 3rd, 5th and 8th Corps—was only practicable, he declared, up to 3 p.m. on the 2nd, since strong reinforcements were being rapidly pushed up to the Allies at Novara.

The result arrived at was a compromise, in that, for the present the army was only ordered to retreat behind the Ticino.

Moltke does not appear altogether to share von Caemmerer's views as to the advantages of a retirement, for he considers that 90,000 men might well have been concentrated on June 1 at Mortara ready to assume the offensive against Palestro and Olengo. The situation of the enemy invited such a measure, and if the retention of the right bank of the Ticino was intended, no other course was possible. If the worst befell, the Austrians possessed a number of fortified crossings by which to fall back, or even the entrenched position at Mortara in their rear; while even if pressed back to Pavia the ground about there was very favourable to the employment of their numerous cavalry for covering their retreat.

To the objection that the Allies at Palestro stood on the flank of any Austrian movement on Novara, it is pointed out that this flank was protected by the Agogna and by the Austrian troops at Robbio. The French were certainly already nearer to Milan than were their enemies; all the more reason then for a speedy termination of the situation, which could be more quickly arrived at by the right than by the left bank.

CHAPTER 6

The Battle of Magenta

In order that the operations of June 4, which are known as the Battle of Magenta, may be properly understood, it will be as well to give some description of the ground on the left bank of the Ticino.

Between the river and the village of Magenta there is first a flat plain for a mile and a half, then a steep irregular bank, some sixty feet high, with a flat table-land on the top; the former is intersected by numerous irrigating channels and belts of trees and bushes, the latter is cultivated for vines and corn with young fruit trees planted very closely together. The railway and post road run very straight across the plain and are liable to be swept by artillery fire from the high ground, all along which, at the edge of the bank, there are favourable positions for guns.

The plateau which skirts the Ticino on its left bank, runs from Turbigo down to Buffalora parallel to the course of the river. At Buffalora the ridge makes a sweep away from the river for a quarter of a mile, after which it again resumes its original direction. In this it continues for about a mile and a half, and then throws out a spur towards the river, behind which lies the village of Ponte Vecchio.

Thus from Buffalora to Ponte Vecchio a semi-circle of positions is formed, facing the river and about one and a quarter miles in length. The breadth of the ridge is nowhere more than 200 yards, and beyond it begins the

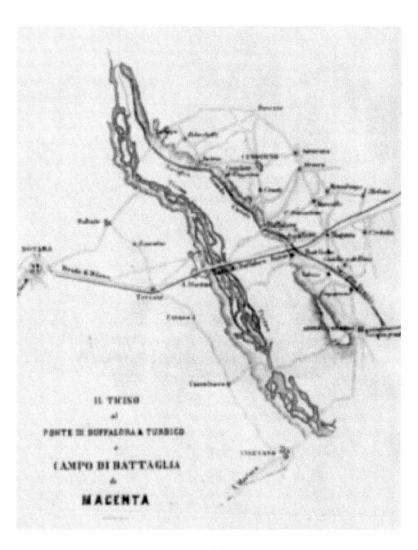

BATTLE OF MAGENTA

ITALIAN ARMY

AUSTRIAN ARMY

Maßstab 1:370000

Franzosen u. Sarden. Österreicher

Kärtchen zur Schlacht bei Solferino (24. Juni 1859).

BATTLE OF SOLFERINO

Lombard plain corresponding to the plain of Novara.

One and a half miles in rear of the ridge lies the village of Magenta; at the latter point converge all the roads coming from that part of the Ticino and unite with the main road, which runs to Milan.

The Grand Canal, which from Turbigo to Buffalora runs at the foot of the ridge, penetrates the latter at the village of Buffalora, and keeps a hundred to a hundred and fifty yards behind it all along this position. The stream runs nearly four miles an hour, and in the neighbourhood of Magenta it has steep banks at each side covered with thorny bushes. Altogether it forms an obstacle quite impassable except at the bridges; of these five must be noticed.

Between the bridge over the Ticino and the ridge there is a space of about a mile of low flat ground, evidently formerly part of the bed of the river, but now canalized and rendered fertile by cultivation. It forms a succession of corn and rice-fields, of which the latter were now under water. Through these low lands two roads led up to the ridge; one, which is the old road to Milan, starts from the left of the present main road and, leading in a succession of bends through the low lands, crosses the ridge and canal just before entering the village of Buffalora. The canal bridge here is completely commanded by the houses of Buffalora, and may be swept by artillery fire from the high ground about the village.

The second bridge over the canal is that of Ponte Nuovo di Magenta, by which the great *chaussée* crosses the canal. This road, starting from the Ticino bridge, slopes gradually down to nearly the level of the high ground which forms the sides of the valley and through which the canal is led. At the canal bridge there are four buildings—one in each angle between the road and the canal; those on the left or east bank of the canal are particularly strongly built and formed in 1859 the Austrian Custom-house.

The railway bridge is about 500 yards below Ponte Nuovo

and crosses the canal at a lower level. The railway, which crosses the Ticino by the same bridge as the *chausée* instead of sinking to the valley as that does, runs on an embankment across it, rising with a uniform, but very gradual gradient to the point where, through a cutting, it enters the high banks which frame in the valley. This long and uniform slope is seen in its whole length from the high ground and lies completely exposed to the fire of guns. At the cutting a quantity of earth had been quarried out to form the embankment over the plain; here a sort of redoubt had been thrown up.

The fourth bridge is Ponte Vecchio di Magenta, near which there is a tolerably large village on both banks of the canal; the part on the right bank consists of older and less substantial buildings than that on the left. There is no direct road to Ponte Vecchio from the Ticino bridge, but roads run along both sides of the canal at the top of the cutting through which it flows from Ponte Nuovo.

The fifth bridge is at Robecco, a large and important village built on both sides of the canal. From Ponte Vecchio downstream the canal becomes shallower and more rapid and its banks are less high and steep. As it gradually diverges from the river, the breadth of the high ground enclosed between it and the low river valley widens gradually from near Buffalora, where it begins to have a breadth of two miles. In cultivation and character the plateau—often called the plateau of Carpenzago—resembles the ground between Turbigo and Magenta. The low ground or valley bed of the Ticino, though not absolutely impassable, is practically unfit for the passage of troops.

On the night of June 3 the positions of the allied forces were as follows:—

The Right: The 1st French Corps and the 1st and 4th Piedmontese divisions at Lumelogno.

The Centre: The 3rd and 4th French Corps, the Cavalry

Divisions Desvaux and Partouneaux and Cassaignolles' brigade of the Cavalry of the Guard at Novara.

The Left: The divisions Mellinet and Camou of the Guard at Trecate and the 2nd Corps at Turbigo.

The Reserve: The 2nd and 3rd Piedmontese infantry divisions and Sambuy's Piedmontese cavalry division at Galliate.

As the Emperor was still uncertain whether Gyulai was concentrating on the right or left bank of the Ticino, he decided to place his army on the line Olengo—Magenta; on the right the 1st Corps to hold the road and rail leading from Mortara to Novara, posted in the strong positions of Olengo and on the Biccoca—occupying more or less the battle-ground of 1849. Baraguey d'Hillier's right to be on the Agogna, where, moreover, he would be supported by Desvaux's cavalry division, while Partouneaux would cover the left of the 1st Corps and maintain communication with the 4th. In the centre the 4th Corps at Trecate and the 3rd at San Martino would watch the roads leading from Vigevano by Sozzago and Cerano to the upper Ticino, and join hands by the Olengo road with the 1st Corps and with the 2nd by the bridges at San Martino. On the left, the 2nd Corps at Magenta would safeguard its own left flank with its brigade of light cavalry and be supported on its right rear by the Guard at Buffalora.

It seemed to Napoleon that whether the Austrians attacked on the left or right bank, he was now strong enough on either to be able to hold his ground until he could transfer to the point threatened the preponderance of strength he undoubtedly possessed, although temporarily debarred from its full use by the river, over which, however, his communications were being hourly improved.

On the night of the 3rd, Mellinet arrived at Trecate, and Espinasse at once rejoined the 2nd Corps in the neighbourhood of Robecchetto.

On the morning of the 4th the different units of the allied army had already marched off to take up the positions assigned to them, when it became known that the Austrians had completely evacuated the left bank, and were moving on Milan; the Emperor then found himself obliged in some degree to modify his earlier dispositions and to thrust forward to engage the enemy those troops which were nearest to him.

The Piedmontese divisions were ordered to cross the river at Turbigo and to follow the steps of MacMahon's corps, while the 3rd and 4th Corps were directed to push on as rapidly as possible and reach the scene of action by way of the passages at San Martino. Circumstances, however, did not allow of the uninterrupted flow of reinforcements to the troops actually in contact with the forces of Count Clam. Of the Piedmontese army only two divisions were able to cross at Turbigo—the 2nd (Fanti) and the 3rd (Durando).

Of these the latter did not reach the scene of the battle at all, while the other—Fanti—only arrived at Mesero at 6 p.m., too late to exert any appreciable influence upon the result of the day's fighting. As a matter of fact the roads and bridges about Turbigo were greatly blocked, while Urban's presence south of Gallarate—menacing the flank and rear of the troops advancing on Magenta—required that one division should show front to him while the other covered the debouchures from the bridges. In like manner the 4th Corps marching from Novara to Trecate, blocked the road by which Canrobert should have reached the Ticino, and he consequently was only able, very late in the day, to bring two brigades into action, while only Vinoy's division of the 4th Corps reached the field at all.

To oppose the Allies the nearest troops were those immediately under the command of Count Clam, and these comprised Urban's three brigades, whatever units of the 1st Corps it had been possible to gather together, the whole of the 2nd Corps, and a portion of the 7th. These numbered 44,780 infantry, 3,803 cavalry and 178 guns, and the various units were on the evening of June 3 disposed as under:—

Of Urban's force the brigade Rupprecht was at Varese with detachments at Somma and Tradate, while the brigades of

Schaffgotsche and Braum (the last detached from the 9th Corps) were respectively south and north of Gallarate.

Cordon's troops had passed the night south of Marcallo, but as the men had practically been without either rest or rations since they arrived from Austria, Clam withdrew them early on the 4th to Magenta, leaving only a very few companies to watch that front.

Burdina (of Montenuovo's division of the 1st Corps) had altogether some seven battalions under his command and was posted on both sides of the canal about Ponte Nuovo and the railway bridge.

Part of Reznicek's brigade of Cordon's division—some 1,500 men—was on the east bank of the canal in and near Buffalora with its right at Bernate.

Of the 2nd Corps Kintzl's brigade was in Robecco with two battalions in Ponte Vecchio on the west bank; the brigades of Szabo, Baltin and Koudelka were in Magenta.

The Cavalry Division was in Corbetta, while the brigades of Gablentz and Lebzeltern, of Reischach's division of the 7th Corps, were near Cerella.

Further off and at Gyulai's disposal were the following: Lilia's division of the 7th Corps—7,600 men with 16 guns—at Castelletto; the 3rd Corps—21,536 men and 56 guns—was at Abbiategrasso, Ozero and Soria; while the 5th Corps, further off still, between Coronate and Besate, numbered 25,092 men and 72 guns, exclusive of the brigade Bils *en route* to Pavia. The 8th and 9th Corps were too far distant for their services to be of any value on this day, but even without them the commander of the Second Army might have been able to count upon some 107,000 infantry, over 5,000 cavalry and 400 guns being available in and about Magenta at some time during June 4.

Against these the Allies could muster in the first line— *viz*.: the Imperial Guard, the 2nd and 3rd Corps— 55,783 infantry, 6,068 cavalry and 144 guns, to hold any Austrian attack in check until the 4th Corps and the divisions of the Piedmontese Army—numbering altogether 73,388 infantry, 4,909 cavalry and 147 guns—should have had time to fall into line with them.

During the night reports came in to Clam from Bernate, that the enemy appeared to be withdrawing from Turbigo and to be moving down stream towards San Martino; as the Austrian outposts in this direction also announced that large numbers of the enemy were gathering on the right bank of the river, the commander of the 1st Corps seems to have come to the conclusion that the main attack would be delivered on the line San Martino—Milan—an impression which was strengthened by reports from the cavalry sent out to the north, who stated—even up to quite late on the morning of the 4th—that Cuggiono and Inveruno were clear of the enemy.

At 9.15 a.m., however, Bernate reported that the strength of the allied force about Turbigo appeared to be increasing, and Clam accordingly ordered forward Baltin's brigade of Herdy's division of the 2nd Corps to Buffalora. This brigade was there drawn up facing both west and north—at Buffalora along the canal as far as Bernate and thence fronting the north on the line Bernate—Casate—Mesero. The canal bridge at Buffalora was now at once blown up, apparently without orders from superior authority; a 6-pounder was placed behind the ruined bridge, seven others being in reserve in the village; while four 12-pounders were placed on the plateau at the northern exit from Buffalora.

At 9.45 Clam reported as follows to Gyulai:

Two strong columns are advancing against the stone bridge over the Ticino and five other columns have been reported on the Novara-San Martino road; these appear to be the Imperial Guard. At Ponte Nuovo, at the railway bridge and in Buffalora I have nine battalions of infantry, five 12-pounders and eight rockets, while at Robecco and Ponte Vecchio there is now Kintzl's brigade. In the event of an attack upon Magenta, I shall send a brigade of the

2nd Corps to Buffalora, keeping the other two brigades of that corps and Reznicek's of the 1st in reserve near Magenta, The Cavalry Division remains at Corbetto sending out strong patrols towards Cuggiono and Inveruno.

He then reports Cordon's overthrow on the previous day and winds up by saying that

the enemy do not seem to have crossed in strength at Turbigo, although fresh reports point to some increase in the hostile forces at that point.

On receipt of this message Gyulai directed Reischach's division of the 7th Corps to move *via* Corbetto on Magenta, where he should act as a support to Cordon and where he would receive further instructions from Clam. At the same time Clam was directed to make use of the divisions of Cordon and Reischach to attack such of the Allies as had already crossed at Turbigo and drive them back; if, however, the enemy were in too great force.

Clam was to break off the action and take up a defensive position about Magenta in view of recommencing the action on the morrow with greatly increased numbers and with a proportionately better hope of success. By this time however, that this message reached its destination, fighting had already broken out on the main road at the eastern end of the Ticino bridge, and Clam then considered that the instructions therein contained could no longer be carried into execution.

Mellinet had been ordered to leave Trecate at 8 a. m. For San Martino in order there to cover the construction of a pontoon bridge which was to be thrown across Ticino just above the stone bridge; 2nd brigade (Wimpffen) [1] left first and it and was followed two hours later by Mellinet himself with his 1st brigade (Cler.) Wimpffen reached the river about 10, and perceiving Austrian riflemen on the left bank, he at once passed over several companies

---

1. It should be remembered that two Austrian commanders also bore this name: the commander of the First Army at Solferino and a brigade commander in Schaffgot-schen's Corps.

and two guns—the latter being carried across by hand—and, covered by these advanced troops, the rest of the 2nd brigade crossed over and took up a position on the further side.

Here the skirmishers of either force became at once engaged while Wimpffen's two guns also came into action, opposing two Austrian pieces which were in battery a few hundred paces from the canal bridge on the west bank, and which together with the Austrian skirmishers, fell back behind the canal, when Wimpffen was able to push forward small parties to Buffalora and Ponte Nuovo.

Mellinet now arrived upon the scene and having received strict orders from the Emperor not to become seriously engaged until MacMahon's attack was developed on the left, he directed Wimpffen to recall his troops and to maintain his position on the east bank some 500 yards in front of the bridge.

At this moment, however, the Emperor, who had just arrived at the junction of the Buffalora and Magenta roads, heard heavy musketry fire from the north, and concluding that MacMahon must now be seriously engaged, he ordered Mellinet to attack and endeavour to carry the villages of Ponte Nuovo and Buffalora.

It will be as well now to see what occasioned the firing which led to the renewal of Mellinet's attack.

MacMahon had been instructed by the Emperor to leave his bivouacs at 9 a.m., and at that hour his 1st Division (La Motterouge) left Robecchetto by the Buffalora road. About midday the division, accompanied by MacMahon in person, had passed through Cuggiono and found the Austrians deployed in front of Casate. The Turcos at the head of the division attacked at once and captured the village, the enemy retiring through Bernate, where they were rallied. Bernate too was carried in the same way with a rush, and the Austrians fell back upon Buffalora with the Turcos in close pursuit. In spite of MacMahon's orders to halt at two hundred yards from the village to give time for the arrival of the whole division, the Turcos pushed on; some of their leading companies rushed on the heels of the fugitives into the outskirts of Buffalora and into an entrenchment to the east of the village, while two companies of the 2nd battalion seized a house close to the canal.

The 3rd battalion remained in reserve. The 4th regiment of the line followed escorting the divisional artillery, some of the guns of which were brought into action on the little plateau of Bernate, and engaged two of Baltin's batteries at a range of about 1,200 yards. The 2nd brigade (de Polhès) was formed up rather on the left rear of the foremost troops midway between Bernate and Marcallo.

Camou's division of the Guard, following La Motterouge, debouched from Casate and took post in rear of the 1st Division, the left of which was covered by the cavalry of General Gaudin de Villaine, who was directed to keep touch with MacMahon's 2nd Division under Espinasse.

This general had been ordered to move on Magenta by Castano, Buscate, Inveruno, Mesero and Marcallo, and reached the first-named village at 11.15, when, expecting shortly to come in touch with the enemy, he halted and deployed for attack from column of route. His 1st brigade (Gault) was moved off to and opened out in the fields on the right of the road, while his 2nd (de Castagny) was in echelon on the left of the road, which was given up to the artillery, and finally a dense cloud of skirmishers covered the left flank of the division . Arrived at Inveruno there was another halt, and it being found that passage across the fields was no longer practicable, the whole column again took to the road, and it was 1.30 p.m. before the advance guard reached Mesero, where it was met by a heavy fire and where Espinasse made preparations for attack.

Wimpffen's renewed attack had by now been launched: of his brigade, the 3rd regiment of grenadiers advanced along the foot of the railway embankment, while the 2nd regiment moved upon Buffalora; the whole of the 1st brigade of the same division was not as yet available, but its regiment of *zouaves* was massed to the left of the Buffalora road, while a battalion of the 1st Grenadiers formed the reserve. It was about 1.30; the 3rd

Grenadiers moved straight upon the small work which covered the railway bridge and stormed over the parapet, turning out the defenders, who fled to the further bank of the canal leaving the railway bridge in the hands of the French. But those of the Austrians who were holding the houses of Ponte Nuovo now poured a heavy fire into the rear of the open work; at this moment the supporting battalion of the 3rd Grenadiers came up and turning sharply to the left it moved up the canal bank, and engaged under cover of the trees and brushwood, covering this part of the field, the Austrians holding the village.

Ponte Nuovo was, however, occupied in considerable strength, the bank and buildings about the road and railway bridges being defended by Burdina's battalions, supported by Szabo's brigade, and it was as much as the French could do to hold on to the ground they had gained. At this moment Cler, commanding Mellinet's 1st brigade, was directed to advance; his *zouaves* rushed forward with great *élan* and carried the bridge and the houses adjoining it, the *zouaves* and the grenadiers pursuing the Austrians, who fell back in some confusion upon Szabo's brigade. It was here that General Burdina fell mortally wounded.

The road and railway bridges were thus in possession of the French; on the left, however, matters had not gone so well. Arriving in front of Buffalora the 2nd Grenadiers found that the bridge had been destroyed and that the houses on the east bank were occupied in strength by the greater part of two battalions of Baltin's brigade, and here all onward movement by the French was temporarily checked.

It was 2 p.m.: Gyulai had just now reached Magenta and learnt of the outcome of the fighting at the canal bridges, and he at once ordered up Reischach's division to retake Ponte Nuovo. Passing through Magenta, the division formed in two lines; in front was Gablentz's brigade, its left covered towards Buffalora by a battalion of Szabo's brigade, while in rear were the battalions of Lebzeltern. The advance of these fresh troops was heralded and prepared by the fire of four guns. Before, however, Reischach's troops could enter into the fight the situation had become worse for the Austrians.

The rapid advance of Cler's brigade had taken Szabo in flank, and these troops—which had already on a previous occasion been severely handled—fell back upon Magenta, so closely followed by the *zouaves* that the defence of Magenta was hurriedly taken in hand. On the north of the main road Liechtenstein had brought up three battalions of Koudelka's brigade, which engaged the French at this point, but they were gradually forced back behind the track connecting Buffalora with the main road. The French had now several battalions and four guns on the east bank of the canal and on either side of the road, and it appeared as though there was nothing to prevent their unopposed march upon Magenta.

It was at this time that Reischach advanced upon Ponte Nuovo and that the fresh troops thus introduced into the fight sufficed to at least check the French advance. Three of Gablentz's battalions fell upon the left of the *zouaves*, drove them back upon the guns and captured one which was in action on the north side of the road. General Cler was killed, the French were repulsed, and in spite of the efforts of a handful of *chasseurs à cheval* of the Guard, who repeatedly charged the Austrian flank, the grenadiers and zouaves were forced back fighting to the houses of Ponte Nuovo. But the losses of the Austrians had not been slight; Reischach himself had been wounded, and Gablentz halted to reform his scattered troops before continuing to press his advantage. This delay was enough to change again the issue of the combat and to give time for the entry into the fight, first of Picard's brigade of the 3rd Corps and later of those of Martimprey and La Charrière of the 4th.

At this critical moment, when the French in this part of the field had fallen back before the Austrian reinforcements, the distant sounds of gun and rifle fire which had been heard beyond Buffalora, and which had decided the Emperor to launch Mellinet to the attack, had unaccountably died down. MacMahon seeing and hearing nothing of Espinasse on his left, and fearing for the result of an attack upon him, while unsupported, by the forces he had found in his front, had given orders that the Turcos should be recalled from before Buffalora and that the artillery should cease fire.

The guns withdrew to Bernate and de Polhès' brigade extended in their front, while Lefebvre strung his brigade out to the left to endeavour to gain touch with the right of MacMahon's 2nd Division. In the meantime Espinasse was continuing his leisurely advance; his 1st brigade (Gault) occupied Marcallo, Reznicek's battalions retiring before it, and here Espinasse intended again to halt, occupying the village with his 1st brigade, while his 2nd was coming up in rear. He proposed to leave his convoy in the village, and seems to have been under the impression that he was being closely followed by the divisions of the Piedmontese Army.

Once concentrated, it was his intention to advance direct upon Magenta. Happily at this moment MacMahon himself rode up and ordered Espinasse to take ground more to his right so as to join on to La Motterouge—keeping his extreme left only on Marcallo. After leaving Marcallo, however, both brigades—now in line—seem to have slightly brought up their left shoulders, since Marcallo was now beyond Castagny's left and both were fronting rather inwards—that is towards the angle of the canal and the main road. In rear of the two divisions of the 2nd Corps, Camou had formed his division in line of battalion columns at deploying intervals. To Castagny's left front, Mensdorff's cavalry guarded the Milan road, while Lilia's division of the 7th Corps had reached and occupied Corbetta on the line of retreat.

It was about 3.30 p.m. when the head of Renault's division of the 3rd French Corps reached the canal where the Guard was holding on to the houses of Ponte Nuovo on the right bank and to the railway buildings. Wimpffen had succeeded in preventing Gablentz from crossing the bridge and retaking the entrenchment, but Wimpffen was now menaced by a regiment of Kintzl's brigade which was moving up the right bank from Carpenzago and Ponte Vecchio to take him in flank. Picard's brigade now came up and entered the entrenchment just as Kintzl's men arrived at the southern parapet.

These were greeted with a murderous fire and the Frenchmen then, pouring tumultuously over the earthworks, drove the enemy before them as far as the nearest buildings of Ponte Vecchio, where further pursuit was checked by the timely destruction of the bridge over the canal. His right being thus cleared, Wimpffen added Picard's remaining battalions to his own, still struggling for foothold, and managed to seize and retain a small group of farm buildings situated to the south of the railway line and about 600 yards beyond the canal. In like manner the houses on the left bank were recaptured and held—in spite of the efforts of one of Lebzeltern's regiments—and three batteries of the artillery of the Guard, taking up a position about Ponte Nuovo, seemed by their fire to assure its possession to the French.

Reischach's men were, however, not yet finished with: his left wing, strengthened by Szabo's brigade, again charged forward; the farm was retaken by the Austrians, and the defenders were driven back to the canal bank. The debouchures of the bridges on the main road and railway were still in the hands of the French, but the troops were greatly exhausted by the continuous fighting, and it was feared that a fresh attack might effect their overthrow, when about 4.45 General Niel arrived on the scene with Martimprey's brigade of Vinoy's division.

Two of these fresh battalions were at once sent forward to the recapture of the farm, and the rest of the brigade, under Martimprey, was ordered to push on to Magenta; La Charrière now appearing with three battalions, he was directed to send two in support of Picard and with the other to follow those attacking the farm.

While the French right wing was thus struggling to assure the passage of the approaches to the main road to the capital, the left wing under MacMahon was once again in action.

Returning from Espinasse to La Motterouge, MacMahon ordered this division to move straight upon Buffalora, and Lefebvre's brigade was soon visible upon the high ground just north of that village. By this time—it was nearly 4 p.m.—some men of the 2nd Grenadiers had swum across the canal, a temporary bridge had been thrown over, and Baltin, seeing that there was some danger of his being crushed between Wimpffen and La Motterouge, evacuated Buffalora and fell back upon Cascina Nuova—rather less than midway between Buffalora and Magenta. Thus when Lefebvre's men entered Buffalora from the north, they found that it had just been occupied by Mellinet's grenadiers.

In the hope of being able to isolate and fall upon one of the two Turbigo columns. Clam now brought Baltin's brigade across towards Marcallo, and these battalions—uniting with those of Reznicek and a stray battalion from Koudelka's brigade—attacked Castagny. The leading French battalions were easily thrown back, but the Austrian movement upon Marcallo, defended by Gault, was beaten back and the Austrians retired upon Magenta.

While fighting was thus going on along the whole semi-circle, a fresh Austrian attack from the south, menaced once more the possession of the canal bridge and main road. When Gyulai ordered up Reischach to retake Ponte Nuovo, he had himself then ridden off to Robecco to hasten the advance and direct the attack of the 3rd Corps. Arrived there, he ordered Schwartzenberg to advance on Ponte Vecchio by both banks of the canal with his whole force. Ramming, accordingly, led his brigade by the east bank and moved upon Ponte Vecchio, Hartung followed on the west of the canal, while still further out to the west Wetzlar conducted his men across the swamps and rice-fields of the Ticino valley in the endeavour to cut the French communications at the San Martino bridge. In rear of all followed Dürfeld's brigade supporting Hartung on the right bank of the Grand Canal.

The French also had received a small reinforcement for the desperate fighting which was about to be reopened for the possession of Ponte Vecchio: Jannin's brigade of Renault's division had just crossed the river and was moving along the main road.

By now Vinoy had succeeded in recapturing the farm buildings to the south of the railway and was moving upon Ponte Vecchio, from the attack on which—on the western bank—Picard had just fallen back. The arrival now of Schwartzenberg's corps made matters once more serious, and by Hartung's advance Picard was driven back to the entrenchment at the bridge.

All efforts of both combatants seemed to be now concentrated on Magenta and Ponte Vecchio, where it appeared the final issue would be fought out. Reznicek occupied the northern outskirts of Magenta; what was left of Baltin's brigade, with the battalions driven from Cascina Nuova, was falling back upon the same point to reform; on the Magenta road Martimprey was driving Gablentz and Lebzelteyn before him, and Szabo was retiring on Magenta where Koudelka and Burdina's brigades had already taken up positions. On either side of the canal Schwartzenberg's infantry was preparing to assault Ponte Vecchio; Ramming and Dürfeld were marching up the east bank to oppose Vinoy, while Wetzlar, unable to cross the swamps by the Ticino, was moving nearer to the canal.

When the brigades of Espinasse hurled back the attack of Baltin and Reznicek on the French left, they followed up the Austrians almost to within view of the town of Magenta, but here—taking post behind the railway embankment—the Austrians were able to rally, and the French battalions, failing to make any impression upon their adversaries, found themselves once more compelled to fall back. But Clam seemed now unaccountably to have renounced any attempts against the French left, and recalled the troops of the 1st and 2nd Corps to the defence of Magenta itself. During the pause which now ensued MacMahon reformed his line of battle and bringing round his right, directed La Motterouge upon Cascina Nuova, whose walls and outbuildings were then still held by the three battalions which had retired from Buffalora; while on either flank of the buildings stood fragments of Szabo's, Baltin's and Lebzeltern's brigades.

Upon this farm now converged the attack of several battalions; the 45th Regiment of the line, on the right of MacMahon's 1st Division, rushed upon it with the bayonet, while several companies of Martimprey's column joined also in the assault. Cascina Nuova was captured and here some 1,500 prisoners were taken. There was now no obstacle between the 2nd Corps and Magenta; La Motterouge was ordered to attack from the direction of Buffalora, Espinasse from Marcallo, while Camou, deployed in rear of the two, was to support both attacks.

It was now 6.30 p.m.: Espinasse formed his leading brigade in two columns; he himself accompanied that which moved direct upon Magenta by the Marcallo road, while Gault—circling round to the east—was to approach Magenta from the Milan direction; Castagny's brigade followed Espinasse more slowly and at some distance in rear. Magenta was ill-adapted for defence; by the gradual pressure applied by MacMahon, the Austrians were forced from the outworks and driven to the houses of the little town.

Within its walls all was confusion; scattered detachments of all arms and of every unit filled each street and open space, while some troops of the 1st and 2nd Corps had already passed hurriedly through the town and retired on Corbetta. On the right of La Motterouge, Martimprey had rapidly pushed on at the head of two battalions and, crossing the railway, he entered upon a desperate struggle for the possession of the church and cemetery, in the course of which the general himself was seriously wounded and his battalions lost half their effectives.

After a protracted struggle Vinay had captured Ponte Vecchio but had been driven out by Dürfeld's brigade, and altogether the possession of this village changed hands some six times. On all sides fresh troops were reaching the field; the head of the 5th Austrian Corps was in sight; Bataille's brigade of the 3rd (Canrobert's) Corps had arrived at the Ticino; Fanti's division of the Piedmontese Army was now visible on the high ground north of Marcallo. The French artillery, however, was now gaining the upper hand; General Auger had succeeded in establishing a long line of guns on the left bank of the canal and had brought the whole ground between Ponte Vecchio and Magenta under a heavy fire.

Towards 7.30 o'clock Espinasse ordered the final advance of his division upon Magenta, and his two columns entering from the north and east, while La Motterouge, closely followed by Camou, penetrated from the west, bloody fighting took place—in the streets, in the churches and from house to house. Here General Espinasse was killed. The Austrians were driven from the town and fell back in great confusion upon Corbetta, covered by Lilia, by Mensdorff, and by Lippert of the 8th Corps who had at this moment reached the scene of action.

About Ponte Vecchio, however—on the left bank—the battle still raged. Ramming, having thrown a battalion into the village, had marched on Magenta, but Schwartzenberg's remaining brigades were fighting hard for victory. The village was captured and recaptured; Vinoy was driven out by the Austrians, and they in turn were driven out by him, and at times portions of Ponte Vecchio were in possession of both combatants.

On the right bank, too, the tide of battle rose and fell; the arrival of reinforcements gave a fleeting success first to one side, then to the other; at one time it seemed that here at least victory would crown the splendid efforts of Hartung and Dürfeld, when the French finally flung two fresh battalions into the fight and secured success for the Allies in this portion also of the bloody field. Wetzlar's attack was paralysed by the heavy fire of the French, and the Austrians fell back in some disorder upon Robecco, closely followed by their adversaries, whose pursuit was, however, checked by the brilliant efforts and repeated charges of the 10th Austrian Hussars over ground quite unsuited to the action of cavalry. Marshal Canrobert himself was nearly captured by these gallant horsemen.

In the battle the losses of the combatants were as follows:—

	Killed.	Wound.		Killed.	Wound.	Miss.
Fr.. Offic.	52	194	Rank and File.	655	3,029	665.
Aust. „	64.	221.	„ „	1,304	4,137	4,500.

(Those shown as "missing" among the Austrians included prisoners.) The *Times* correspondent with the Allies states that all the French and many of the Austrian wounded had been removed during the night, but on the third day after the battle some were found lying about the field and brought in. This was owing in a great measure to the idea which had been inculcated in the Austrian soldiers, that the Allies ill-treated and killed the wounded; so they hid themselves, thinking the chances of starving preferable to certain death. Numbers concealed themselves in the cellars of the houses of Magenta and in the farmhouses near which they had been wounded.

On this night the French and Piedmontese bivouacked practically where the close of the battle found them; Renault (3rd Corps) and Vinoy (4th) at Ponte Vecchio on either side of the canal, where they were joined during the night by the divisions of Trochu and Bourbaki of the 3rd Corps. Of the Imperial Guard, Mellinet was at Buffalora and Ponte Nuovo, Camou was in rear of Magenta, while the whole of the 2nd Corps occupied the town. The remaining two divisions of the 4th passed the night at Trecate, the 1st Corps at Olengo; while of the Piedmontese divisions, Fanti was at Marcallo and the others at Turbigo and Galliate. The Imperial Headquarters was at San Martino, that of Victor Emmanuel at Villa Fortuna.

Of the Austrian corps the 1st, 2nd, and 7th were in or about Corbetta and Cerella, the 3rd and 5th were at Robecco, Mensdorff at Bareggio, and Headquarters at Abbiategrasso; the nearest unit of the 8th Corps was at Bestazzo, and the 9th Corps was still south of Pavia.

During the whole of the 4th, Urban had done nothing beyond assisting to delay—by the mere fact of the presence of two of his brigades south of Gallarate—the advance of the Piedmontese divisions. His instructions, however, had been of the vaguest, for all that he had been told was that Clam, if he considered it advisable, would attack the Allies at Turbigo, but that if on the other hand he retired on Magenta, Urban should take the opportunity of striking at the flank of the French, were they then to advance.

About midday on the 4th, Urban learnt from the commander of a detachment which he had placed at Ferno, that fighting appeared to be going on south of Cuggiono, but that touch could not be established with the troops of the 1st Corps. Urban now moved the two brigades with him by Busto Arsizio and Vanzaghello to beyond Magnano where he remained for the rest of the day, unable to advance and yet making no attempt to rejoin the main army.

A consideration of the numbers actually engaged on either side [2] seems to prove that a battle was not anticipated on the 4th, either by the Allies or by the Austrians. It appears to be clear that the situation was not thoroughly appreciated by the Austrian commander-in-chief, and that he was drawn into a general action through not supporting at the outset, and with sufficient forces, the lieutenant who had been surprised by the advance of MacMahon.

By the morning of the 4th, Gyulai knew that a crossing had already been effected at Turbigo and that there was nothing to prevent the passage of the Trecate columns (already reported) at San Martino. Had then the bridges over the canal at Bernate, Buffalora, Ponte Nuovo and Ponte Vecchio been destroyed—and Clam had already on the night of the 2nd given orders that all of them were to be prepared for demolition—the junction of the two French columns must have been greatly hindered and delayed, and Gyulai might have had time to array largely superior forces between Marcallo and Buffalora to oppose MacMahon; might have watched the line of the Grand Canal with comparatively few troops; and could himself have moved in strength, by Robecco and Carpenzago, against the flank of the allied columns crossing at San Martino.

Rüstow suggests the following dispositions for the morning of the 4th (it being accepted that the canal bridges, except that at Robecco, had by then been all destroyed): one of Clam's divisions at Cuggiono to check the advance of the Turbigo column; Liechtenstein's corps to hold the canal line with weak detach-

2. French, 48,090 men and 87 guns; Austrians, 61,618 men and 176 guns.

ments at Bernate, Buffalora, Ponte Nuovo and Ponte Vecchio, the remainder in reserve on the *chaussée*; another of Clam's divisions and Zobel's corps as main reserve in Magenta, for employment when necessary against MacMahon; while Schwartzenberg's corps at Robecco to be held in readiness to strike at the flank of the San Martino columns—whence too it could be drawn in to Magenta should it be found impossible to prevent the junction of the allied forces.

In a letter published in a German newspaper shortly after the war, and generally attributed to Count Gyulai, the following statement occurs:

> The battle of Magenta was in no way an accident. When the Austrian Commander gave up the advantage offered by his excellent position at Robbio and Mortara against the oblique line of operations of the enemy, and when he had, as a consequence of this, also renounced all idea of the indirect defence of the Ticino by Pavia and Bereguardo, he decided on a direct defence behind the river. This could be carried out in two ways; either from a position outside the Milan-Magenta road or by a flank attack—of the same nature as the one from Mortara based on Pavia and Bereguardo—against the line Vercelli—— Novara.

The first of these alternatives was, he says, rejected, because in case of a reverse a retreat must have been made by Milan and Brescia. It was proposed then to remain in the vicinity of the Po to occupy with the help of the points Vaccarizza, Piacenza, Brescia and Borgoforte interior lines between the forces of the enemy in the north and those approaching from the south. It was also decided, on giving up the Lomellina, to make a flank movement against the line Novara—Milan. Gyulai then suggests that when this retreat commenced on June 2, the orders given to the different corps had provided for the offensive being assumed against the enemy's flank whenever opportunity offered, and for retirement, if necessary, behind the Abbiategrasso-Milan canal.

He hints that the sudden intervention of Hess upset these

plans, and that the army thus reached its positions late and assumed a formation which had not been intended, with the result that the battle commenced and was sustained, not—as had been planned—by the whole army, but by a portion of it only.

Moltke insists that the Austrians should under no circumstances have joined battle on the 4th. The Allies would certainly have been able to complete their passage of the river undisturbed, but this could not by then have been prevented. He considers that all was not then lost, for if the Austrians had only concentrated somewhere north of the Abbiategrasso-Milan canal, the Allies must have attacked them before marching on Milan.

One primary condition however, for not fighting on the 4th was that the Austrians should under no circumstances be drawn into a premature action; if Clam was attacked, he should have been withdrawn towards Abbiategrasso. Moltke maintains that neither the French nor the Austrians intended to fight at Magenta, and that the Austrians permitted themselves to be drawn into the action through supporting Clam. If, however, they stood to fight at Magenta, they should have fought behind the line of the canal, since the river and canal were so close together that if an attempt were made to hold both, the canal must follow the loss of the river line. The position, too, behind the canal was the more commanding, could have been held by fewer troops, and would have permitted of larger forces being employed against Turbigo.

Even as late as the morning of the 4th when he was already engaged, Clam should have been recalled, and the decisive action postponed until the day following. Kuhn, the Austrian chief of the staff, calculates that on the 5th the Austrians would have had a superiority of 45,000 men with 290 guns, and, according to Moltke, the night of the 4th was for Napoleon a very anxious one. He must have known that he had only been engaged with a portion of the Austrian Army, and that even that, though defeated, remained in threatening proximity. The whole of Gyulai's force could be brought up next day to renew the action, and this, as we shall see, was actually decided upon.

A considerable portion of the allied army was still on the right bank, while the passage at San Martino on the exposed flank might well have been endangered by an Austrian success in the morning about Ponte Nuovo. All that night the Allies were passing infantry and artillery over the river in readiness for accepting battle next day under the best possible conditions.

Von Caemmerer thoroughly approves of the decision to strike at the allied flank between the Ticino and Magenta, but finds serious fault with the execution, and especially with the ever present idea that an attack by the Allies in the front had still to be guarded against. He rightly complains of the multiplicity and excessive detail of the orders issued by the Austrian Headquarter Staff to subordinate commanders, but he finds fault with Gyulai for not giving Clam precise directions as to which side of the canal he was to take his stand.

On neither side in this battle did everything fall out quite as had been arranged or intended, but on the battle- field the French certainly displayed superior fighting powers, as their leaders showed better generalship. On the other side the Austrians were brought piecemeal into action; there seemed at times something almost like a reluctance to engage; and throughout reserves were kept far too much in hand—caution, as on previous occasions, prevailing over enterprise.

CHAPTER 7

The Action at Melegnano

At 8.30 p.m. on the night of the battle, Gyulai—who at that hour was still in Robecco—issued orders for the renewal of the action on the morrow. The 3rd Corps was directed to hold on to Robecco at all costs, the 5th Corps being placed in rear of the village in support; Schwartzenberg was given the command of both these corps. The 1st, 2nd, 7th, and 8th Corps were directed to hold the position about Corbetta, and these were all placed at the disposal of Count Clam. Schwartzenberg's line of retreat was by Abbiategrasso, that of Clam by Gaggiano. Shells were still falling in Robecco while these orders were being dispatched, and Army Headquarters withdrew to Abbiategrasso, where the details of the operations of the next day were worked out.

From a fragmentary order—which was then drawn up but does not appear to have ever reached the 3rd Corps, for which it was intended—it seems that Gyulai's intentions were something as follows: in the event of the Allies moving forward in the morning, he proposed remaining altogether on the defensive until they should debouch from Magenta, when he intended falling upon them with the whole of his reserves—driving them back and endeavouring to enter Magenta with them. The Austrian commander-in-chief gives no hint as to what was likely to be the result of the possible recapture of Magenta, and then proceeds to issue instructions as to retreat upon the line of the Abbiategrasso-Milan canal, should a retirement become necessary.

Late that night, Melczer, who was commanding in Milan, was ordered to evacuate the capital, sending all munitions and supplies by rail to Verona and the troops to Lodi, whither also any of Clam's oncoming troops were to be directed; the railway bridge over the Adda at Cassano was to be destroyed.

At the time that these orders were in course of preparation, Gyulai seems to have had no conception of the degree of demoralization of some of the units under his command. Clam had just dispatched a staff officer to Army Headquarters conveying a report of the deplorable condition of the portion of the army under his orders, when, about midnight, he received Gyulai's instructions relative to the renewal of the battle on the morrow. Clam then sent off the following statement, which reached Abbiategrasso about 1.30 a.m. on the 5th, and which—together with one of similar purport and couched in much the same terms from Zobel—decided Gyulai to renounce all idea of resuming the offensive:

I have this moment—11.45 p.m.—received from Rittmeister Zichy the general orders for tomorrow and feel myself urgently compelled to state that it is quite impossible that the instructions therein contained can be carried out, since their execution would only result in the complete and irreparable ruin of the army. Some of the troops are so absolutely disorganised that a complete company— far less a whole battalion—cannot be got together.[1] Many days are required for rallying. The troops of all units are completely mixed up and scattered in different places. The only way to save the army is to retreat as quickly as possible. Under these circumstances it is quite impossible for me to comply with the instructions received, and I shall therefore continue before dawn the retirement on Binasco which I have already ordered. I have made dispositions to this end as far as can be done, and it is impossible for me to countermand them. I therefore urgently and humbly

1. 47 officers and 3,411 men of seven different regiments had retired direct on Milan, besides individuals of other corps.

request that the orders now received may be cancelled.

At 3 a.m. then on the 5th, Army Headquarters issued the following orders for the retreat:—

The 3rd Corps to move by Abbiategrasso to Morimondo on the 5th, and to Pavia on the 6th.

The 5th Corps on the 5th to Fallavecchio and Basiano and next day to Fossarmato.

The 7th Corps to Rosate and Gudo Visconti on the 5th, and on the 6th to Campo Morto and Gualdrasco.

The 2nd Corps to move on the 5th by Guggiano to Tainate, and on the following day to Torre Vecchia.

The 7th Corps to Piave on the 5th, and Landriano on the 6th.

[2] The 1st Corps to Piave on the 5th, and Torre Vecchia on the 6th.

The Cavalry Division to move by Bareggio to Gudo Gambaredo on the 5th, and on the next day to Siziano.

Army Headquarters was to be on the 5th at Binasco, and on the 6th at Belgiojoso.

Before, however, any orders regarding the intended retreat had reached the 3rd and 5th Corps, fighting had again broken out at Carpenzago during the early hours of the 5th. Both sides declare that the action was initiated by the attack of the other, but the probability is that it resulted naturally from the propinquity of the advanced troops of both. However this may be, Hartung's brigade of the 3rd Corps advanced from Robecco and vigorously attacked Ponte Vecchio, the 14th Austrian Regiment of infantry—which had already greatly distinguished itself and suffered heavy losses the previous day—advancing with great dash against Bataille's brigade, which found the outposts at Ponte Vecchio.

The French were here, however, in great strength, and the

---

2. It should be noted that this corps was still anything but complete; the brigade Hoditz was in Bergamo, Paszthory between Verona and Milan, and Brunner between Verona and Botzen.

Austrians were repulsed, but were not pursued beyond Robecco.

The Austrian losses in this little affair are not forthcoming in any detail, but they can hardly have been less than those of the French, who admit having had thirteen officers and 216 men killed and wounded.

The French made no organised advance until the 6th, when the Emperor Napoleon threw forward strong columns on either flank—the one to regain touch with the main body of the enemy retreating south, the other to endeavour to cut off Urban, who had been reported to be about Monza. The 3rd and 4th Corps moved accordingly upon Abbiategrasso, which they found to be evacuated and where they learnt that the Austrians were retiring upon Pavia and Lodi, while the 2nd Corps with Desvaux's cavalry and the Piedmontese advanced on Rho and Garbagnate, whence a force of all arms was launched in pursuit of Urban.

We have already seen that this commander had passed the whole of the 4th in a state of hesitation and inactivity, and it was not until the following morning that he made any movement. He then advanced towards Castano and Turbigo, and there at once found himself confronted by the Piedmontese divisions, which had crossed the canal and were moving on Magenta. He then appeared to realize the gravity of the general situation and his own immediate peril, and at once retired to Castegnate, sending orders to Rupprecht to withdraw from Somma and Varese—the troops at Somma to Gallarate and Castegnate, those at Varese to Tradate. On the 6th Urban learnt that Milan and Monza had been evacuated by the Austrians, and he at once fell back with all speed to escape the net which was being spread for him.

MacMahon's 2nd Division (now commanded by Decaen *vice* Espinasse killed in action) moved up from Magenta on Garbagnate, the Piedmontese on San Lorenzo, while Garibaldi—whom recent events had rescued from a somewhat critical situation—descended from Varese by Como and Barlassina; but

Rupprecht's brigade, forming Urban's rearguard, just managed, by hard marching, to slip through the converging forces. During the night of the 6th all three brigades crossed the Lambro at Canonica, and pushing on at daybreak on the 7th made for the Adda by Vimercate.

On the 7th the Allies entered Milan, and early next morning Napoleon and Victor Emmanuel rode in at the head of their victorious armies, receiving a tremendous reception from the Milanese; an eye-witness, however, remarks:

> On seeing this indescribable scene of gratitude, joy, happiness, homage—one might almost say worship—it could not be forgotten that within fifty yards of the scene of this wild enthusiasm is the Casa Creppi, on the balcony of which stood Charles Albert and Victor Emmanuel when, after the disasters of August, 1848, they were fired upon from the crowd below.

On the night of the 7th the Imperial Headquarters was at Quarto Gaguino, the Guard was at Casa Pobietta, the 1st Corps at San Pietro d'Olmo, the 3rd at Gaggiano, the 4th at Corsico, while the Piedmontese were at Nerviano, Parabiago and Lainate, the Royal Headquarters being at the last-named place. The 2nd French Corps was in Milan, while the cavalry divisions of Desvaux and Partouneaux occupied Magenta.

> "There are two great arteries of communication which intersect Lombardy from west to east, from the Ticino to the Mincio, thus forming two chief lines of operation in that country. One is the high road from Ponte di Buffalora to Milan and from thence to Treviglio, Calcio, Brescia and the Mincio; the other more to the south from Pavia by Belgiojoso, Pizzighettone, Cremona and Bozzolo to Mantua. By the flanking movement of the Allies and the battle of Magenta the Austrians were cut off from the first of these two lines and pressed towards this latter, which they have always considered as their chief line of operations. Running as it does in the vicinity of the Po, it has been

provided with a series of strongholds, all of them erected at the passages of the confluents of the Po, which come down from the north almost at right angles to the latter.

The object being to out-manoeuvre rather than to beat the Austrians, who were retreating on the southern line towards the Mincio, the northern was chosen by the Allies for theirs.

Again, keeping the object to be attained in view, nothing could be more appropriate than this choice and the plan based on it. The northern line of operations runs in a straight line, almost to the Mincio, is consequently shorter than the southern, to which besides the Austrians had, under the most favourable circumstances, two marches from Abbiategrasso. Thus there was every possibility of reaching the Mincio line as soon as, if not sooner than, the enemy.

The Austrian troops remained twenty-four hours in the positions which they had been told to reach on the 6th, the outposts occupying a line drawn from the Ticino through Giovenzano and Carpiano; Roden's brigade of the 8th Corps held Melegnano with outposts at San Giuliano on the Milan road, and both Roden and Mensdorff received the strictest orders to push patrols in all directions and right up to the very gates of the capital. The upper Adda about Treviglio was held by the brigades of Hoditz and Brunner.

The Austrian retreat was continued on the 7th as follows:—

8th Corps with four brigades to the right bank of the Adda at Lodi—Roden remaining in Melegnano.
7th Corps to the left bank of the Adda at Lodi.
1st Corps to hold the line of the Adda from Lodi to Treviglio with three brigades of Montenuovo's division, one of these three being Teuchert's, made up from the late garrison of Milan.
Hoditz to hold the line of the railway from Brescia to Gorlago.
The Cavalry Division to Lodi, bivouacking on the left

bank of the Adda on the Pandino road.

All these were placed under the orders of Benedek, commanding the 8th Corps.

The 2nd Corps was to move to Borghetto.

The 3rd Corps, with the troops from Pavia—the latter under General Pokorny—to bivouac between San Angiolo and Bargano: these two corps, with the remainder of the 1st, moving by the same road after crossing the Adda, were placed under Schwartzenberg's command.

The 9th Corps marched to Codogno, while of the 5th one division (Sternberg's) moved to Campo Rinaldo, and Paumgartten's to Santa Cristina.

From the above it will be seen that the retirement of the Austrian Army was to be carried out in three great columns: that on the right, under Benedek, by Lodi, Soncino, Manerbio to Montechiaro; the centre, under Schwartzenberg, by Borghetto, Bertonico and Robecco to Valeggio, Volta and Roverbello; while the third or left column, accompanied by the heavy baggage and other impedimenta, moved by Pizzighettone, Cremona and Piadena towards Mantua. The different columns were directed so to time their marches as to reach their destinations on the 11th and 12th, but the 8th Corps, which was as yet intact, was, with the Cavalry Division, to follow a day's march in rear of the 7th Corps, acting as a rearguard and maintaining touch with the enemy.

Benedek was given the following instructions: in the event of the pursuit not being pressed he was to take up a position about Montechiaro, occupying Ponte San Marco and Calcinate in strength; if, however, he were closely followed, he was to withdraw by Castiglione delle Stiviere behind the Mincio, making towards Valeggio with the bulk of his troops while covering his flank with a small force near Lonato. Should, on the other hand, his retirement by Leno and Montechiaro appear likely to involve him in any danger, he was to use his discretion as to retiring by Asola and Goito.

It was the intention of Gyulai, should the retreat of the Second Army not be molested, to concentrate between Castiglione and Lonato—holding Ponte San Marco and Montechiaro as advanced posts—whence he estimated that the line of the Mincio could best be defended, while retaining one corps for the defence of the lower Chiese and Oglio.

Urban, who had this day regained touch with the main army, was directed to send all his heavy ordnance and other stores to Peschiera under the escort of one of his brigades, which, on completion of this duty, was to return and take up a position on the Chiese at Ponte San Marco and so safeguard the right flank of the army. With his two other brigades Urban was ordered to cross into Valtelin by Edolo and the Aprica pass, crush the revolution which had there broken out and restore order, taking measures at the same time for safeguarding his ultimate retreat into the southern Tyrol by Mount Tonale.

The strength of the garrison of Piacenza was raised, for the Austrian commander-in-chief hoped eventually to use the fortress as the pivot of an energetic offensive, which appeared to Gyulai not to be impossible in view of the serious losses which he believed the French to have suffered at Magenta. Bergamo and Brescia were for the present to be held, the garrison of the former to effect its ultimate retreat by Romano to Antignate. there joining on to Montenuovo's troops from Treviglio, and withdrawing thence to Bagnolo; the troops from Brescia were later on to retreat behind the Chiese, holding the bridges at Ponte San Marco, Calcinato, and Montechiaro.

During the night of the 7th-8th, Gyulai received from the Emperor Franz Josef stringent orders to stand fast on the Adda, or, in the event of that river being already passed in retreat, at least to take up a position on the high ground between Piacenza and Lodi, and upon these orders Gyulai issued very early on the morning of the 8th the following instructions for the resumption of the offensive—instructions which, however, did not reach some units until they had already recommenced their retirement: Pavia, which was already evacuated, was to be re-occupied by one brigade of the 5th Corps, the remaining brigades taking up a position about Corte Olona.

The 3rd Corps was to stand fast at San Angiolo, sending one brigade to Landriano and stretching out a hand to Roden's brigade of the 8th Corps in Melegnano. The 1st and 2nd Corps were to remain in Borghetto, while the 7th and 8th Corps and the Cavalry Division were to halt in Lodi, sending out strong patrols towards Milan, Paullo and Melzo, and establishing a chain of posts on the right bank of the Adda covering the northwest of Lodi. Roden was to place Melegnano in a state of defence and join hands with the brigade in Landriano; the 9th Corps was to concentrate in Codogno; while Bergamo and Brescia were to be held until the army should resume its retreat. The brigades of Hoditz and Brunner were placed at the disposal of Urban, who was now ordered to concentrate his five brigades at Treviglio and Canonica; while Montenuovo was directed to halt on the Adda, with Pandino as his centre, and watch the line of the river from Lodi to the Milan-Treviglio road—if possible, occupying Paullo and sending strong reconnoitring parties to Melzo and Gorgonzola.

Early on the 8th, it becoming apparent that the Allies were advancing towards the Lambro from Milan, Benedek ordered up Boer's brigade from Lodi to support Roden in Melegnano, where Berger, the divisional general, was himself in command. Berger had been instructed to offer resistance only to weak detachments of the enemy, and to fall back before any show of real strength.

The report of the advance of the Allies, and of the measures which Benedek had adopted, reached Army Headquarters in Codogno about 1 p.m., and Gyulai at once issued orders for striking at the enemy's flank on the morrow. The 8th, supported by the 7th Corps, was to hold the enemy at Melegnano, while the 3rd, 1st, and 2nd struck at his right or western flank; the 5th Corps was to advance along the left bank of the Ticino in the direction of Rosate, thus guarding the Austrian left, while the 9th Corps was to form a general reserve at San Angiolo. These dispositions, however, did not commend themselves to Baron

Hess, who considered that any offensive effort was hopeless in view of the numerical superiority of the enemy, and after a long discussion with Gyulai the idea of the offensive was—apparently under some pressure—abandoned.

The Allies seem to have been well informed of the movements of the Austrians, and especially of the occupation of Melegnano by Roden, and of the efforts which that commander was making to put the town in a state of defence. The Emperor Napoleon was, however, unable to satisfy himself whether the intention was merely to cover the further retreat of the Austrians, or whether the town was meant to serve as a base for an offensive movement against Milan. On the evening of the 7th, therefore, Marshal Baraguey d'Hilliers received orders to take steps towards clearing up the situation. The marshal was instructed to endeavour—with the assistance of the 2nd Corps—to intercept the Austrians retiring from Binasco and Landriano on Lodi, and for this purpose he was to move at 4 a.m. on the 8th towards Melegnano, halting either at San Donato or San Giuliano; during the 8th, however, further orders reached Baraguey, under which he was to carry Melegnano the same day. For this purpose MacMahon's [3] corps was placed under his orders, while General Niel was also detailed to support the movement.

Baraguey's 1st Division (the brigades Dieu and Blanchard) having reached San Donato, branched off by Civesio, Viboldone and Mezzano and made for Riozzo, in view of establishing itself at Cerro to cut off the retreat of the Austrians from Melegnano by the right bank of the Lambro. The 2nd Division (the brigades Niel and de Négrier) quitted the main road at San Giuliano and marched down the Lambro by Zivido and San Brera to gain the Austrian right flank; while the 3rd Division (the brigades Goze and Dumont) moved down the main road straight upon Melegnano, but being greatly delayed by the congested state of the road, it was not until 5.45 p.m. that this division arrived within sight of the town. The road by which the 3rd Division moved

---

3. MacMahon had been created a Marshal of France and Duke of Magenta for his share in the victory of the 4th.

was broad and straight and was bordered throughout by wide ditches, crossed here and there by stone bridges leading out to the fields, which were seamed by irrigation cuts and covered with high crops and trees, the field of view being thus greatly restricted.

Roden's brigade had been in occupation of Melegnano since the evening of the 6th, and considerable time and labour had been expended in putting the place in a state of defence; the churchyard lying to the front of the town had walls six feet high, and these had been provided with *banquettes*, while a farm on the opposite side of the main road had been fortified. The *chaussée* itself had been cut and a strong barricade erected across it, and at the northern entrance of the town an earthwork had been thrown up and four guns there placed in position; the walls, too, to the north had all been loopholed.

Melegnano was held by the 2nd and 3rd battalion of the 11th Infantry Regiment—the whole of the 3rd battalion holding the Milan front, while the 2nd gave one company for the defence of the cemetery and half another for that of the farm. Four companies of this regiment guarded the west and south-west towards Landriano. The Grenadier Battalion of the same regiment formed the local reserve, and was posted on the east side of the town. A general reserve, of two battalions, one and a half batteries and a few cavalry, was placed to the southeast of Melegnano in the angle between the Lodi and Mulazzano roads. The out posts which had held the line Mezzano—San Brera—Colturano fell back before the advance of the French columns,

Melegnano is divided by the Lambro into two parts of unequal size; it is, moreover, a very straggling town, formed of groups of detached buildings, making it difficult to defend, and with an old castle in the larger or western portion of the town, surrounded on three sides by a moat.

About 6 p.m. Baraguey ordered Bazaine (3rd Division) to attack; a company of zouaves extended on either side of the main road, and two guns came into action on the *chaussée* itself, engaging the Austrian guns behind the earthwork. Very soon

Bazaine—considering that the vigour of the Austrian artillery fire was slackening—prepared to assault; the knapsacks were thrown down on the road, three companies of *zouaves* deployed to the right, followed by two battalions of the 34th Regiment of the line, while the remainder of the zouaves, supported by the 33rd, charged up the road straight at the barricade. The French artillery ceased firing, and the 2nd Brigade—halting at the spot where the road had been cut—remained in reserve.

In the meantime the 2nd Division (Ladmirault) had barely reached San Brera when firing was heard on its right; pushing on rapidly, the 10th Battalion of *chasseurs* and the 15th Regiment of the line were soon able to join hands with Bazaine's *zouaves*, and forcing back the Austrians in this quarter, possessed themselves of the outskirts of the town between the river and the San Brera road.

The divisional artillery had accompanied General Forey, and was established about 1,200 yards from the village with infantry on either flank and the rest of the brigade in reserve. The other brigade had just debouched from Mezzano. MacMahon during this time was endeavouring, in accordance with his instructions, to gain the extreme right and rear of the Austrians. His 2nd Division (Decaen) leading, he marched by Linate and Bettola and reached Mediglia about 4 p.m.. La Motterouge—some considerable distance in rear—making for the same spot by Monticello and Carpianello. Decaen moved on Balbiano and was preparing there to halt when the guns of the 1st Corps were heard in action, and he at once resumed his march, pushing on through Dressano with the idea of placing his division astride the Melegnano-Lodi road.

The 4th Corps (Niel) made a wide detour to the west, and the two leading divisions reached and halted at Carpiano, while the third, pushing further south, arrived at Gnignano and threw forward artillery and infantry towards Landriano. Here about 6 p.m. the 4th Corps heard the sound of the firing at Melegnano, but no attempt whatever was made to advance or co- operate further, in the absence of orders other than those issued:

"That the 4th Corps was to be held in readiness to assist the 1st Corps—if required."

Bazaine's leading battalions had now made repeated assaults upon the front of the town; driven back more than once by a murderous fire from the Austrians in the houses and behind the enclosures, the *zouaves* and 33rd returned again and again to the attack; first the cemetery and then the farms were captured and the two main streets were occupied, when Ladmirault, penetrating at the same time from the east, drove in upon Bazaine's men the defenders of that flank. There was desperate fighting hand to hand, the Austrians offering a gallant resistance to overwhelming numbers and nearly capturing in the *mêlée* the Eagle of the 33rd. One of the Austrian guns at the northern entrance of the town was dismounted by a shell and captured by the French, but the others were successfully brought off.

Berger now ordered Roden to evacuate Melegnano covered by Boer's brigade, which had come up and was in position in rear of the town, holding the Casa Bernada and deployed towards Riozzo.

Ladmirault, collecting portions of three of his battalions, sent them towards the Mulazzano road, with orders to cross it and endeavour to cut the Austrian retreat; but these were received by so heavy a fire from Boer's men that they were not able to advance; MacMahon's guns, however, had reached the Mulazzano road more to the east, and were able seriously to harass the final retirement of the Austrians upon Lodi. Roden's brigade passed through that of Boer—who had by now been mortally wounded—and the remains of the two Austrian brigades were able to effect their retreat, practically unmolested, under the cover of a violent rainstorm which had long been threatening, and which now burst over the field.

The French had pushed their attack so quickly that the greater part of the town was already in their hands while many isolated bodies of the enemy were still holding out in the houses and enclosures, and to this circumstance may in large measure be attributed the many captures which were effected. That the brigades under Boer and Roden did well is unquestionable; the French were in six times greater strength, and if the "missing" are left out of count, the Austrians inflicted a greater loss than they themselves suffered, while they were able to draw off without serious hindrance. For this last they were indebted to the failure in combination of the 1st and 2nd Corps and to the extraordinary inaction of Niel, but as Baraguey d'Hilliers states in his report on the action to the Emperor:

Pour que ces combinaisons pussent avoir un plein succès, il fallait que le temps ne manquât pas à leur développement, et, en me prescrivant d'opérer le jour même de mon départ de San Pietro d'Olmo, Votre Majesté rendait ma tâche plus difficile.

The French acknowledge a loss of 153 killed, 734 wounded (seventy officers were killed and wounded) and sixty-four missing, while the Austrian casualties are given as 120 killed, 240 wounded, and 1,114 missing, of whom something over a hundred only were able to rejoin their units a few days after the action.

Of the three French corps engaged at Melegnano, the 1st occupied the town that night; the 2nd bivouacked at Dressano, the 4th at Carpiano; while of the Austrians the 9th Corps, with Army Headquarters, was in Codogno, the 7th and 8th and part of the 1st in Lodi; at Borghetto was the rest of the 1st and the whole of the 2nd, while the 3rd was at San Angiolo and the 5th at Corte Olona.

Moltke does not see that any object whatever was gained by the Austrians standing fast at Melegnano, their action being only justified if they had any intention of moving forward across the Lambro, and there was certainly at this time no idea of resuming the offensive against the concentrated army of the Allies. All the Austrians really needed to do was to halt and endeavour to glean some intelligence of the enemy's movements; it was, above all things, important to avoid just then the moral effect of heavy losses accompanied by defeat.

Lecomte says that to derive any real advantage, the Allies

should have advanced upon Melegnano forty-eight hours earlier, when Lodi and Pizzighettone might well have been for Gyulai what the passage of the Beresina was for the First Napoleon. He blames Baraguey d'Hilliers for assaulting Melegnano and thereby incurring such heavy casualties, pointing out that he was not, as stated in his report on the action, directed to "*chasser l'ennemi de Melegnano*" but to "*intercepter les Autrichiens qui se retirent de Binasco et de Landriano sur Lodi.*" This mission, Lecomte submits, might well have been accomplished by holding Roden in front with a small force, and outflanking him on the left with both the 1st and 2nd Corps.

CHAPTER 8

Austrians Retreat Behind the Mincio

It was stated in the first chapter that on the mobilisation of the "Army of Italy," a 5th Corps had been formed and placed under the command of Prince Napoleon, and that Generals D'Autemarre and Uhrich had been appointed to lead the two divisions of which it was composed. So far but little has been heard of the movements of this corps, to which a special mission had been confided, and it may be as well to give a short account of its operations before proceeding with the narrative of the events in Lombardy subsequent to the action at Melegnano.

Prince Napoleon had disembarked at Genoa on May 12, but the moiety of his command was taken from him, when—within a week of his arrival upon Italian soil—D'Autemarre's division was placed under the orders of the Commander of the 1st Corps, and thenceforth took part in the operations described in the preceding chapters. There only remained, therefore, under the immediate orders of the Prince, Uhrich's division and the cavalry brigade of General Dalmas de Laperouse, and with these troops the Commander of the 5th Corps was directed to re-embark and proceed to Leghorn for the occupation of Tuscany, which had been abandoned by its Grand Duke, and for which protection against the Austrians had been sought by Tuscan envoys sent to the Emperor Napoleon.

The mission confided to the Prince was to effect a diversion in the south and so cause the enemy to divide his forces, and further to preserve the neutrality of the Papal States; it was authoritatively stated that no attempt to violate the territory of the Pontiff would be made by the Allies provided Austria exercised equal consideration. It was also anticipated that the presence in Tuscany of even a weak corps would tend to prevent the Austrians from drawing supplies from Central Italy; while the Prince would be able to assist in the organisation of the military forces of the Duchies. For the furtherance of this end, the Prince was to assume command of the Tuscan troops under General Ulloa and of the various bodies of volunteers under command of General Mezzacapo.

The Prince reached Leghorn on the 23rd, and, three days later, Uhrich's division was disembarked, the mounted troops of Laperouse only arriving on May 30.

The Commander of the 5th Corps occupied the positions to the west of the Apennines with his 2nd brigade (du Bourguet), so as to watch the Duchy of Modena with the assistance of the local troops and volunteers; while the 1st brigade (Grandchamp), with the cavalry, was concentrated in Florence. Reconaissances were pushed in all directions, and the French troops were kept constantly exercised, ready for the part which all hoped they yet might take in the more active work of the campaign.

After the battle of Magenta, Prince Napoleon asked sanction to cross the Apennines and establish touch with the main army of the Allies—driving the Austrians back to the right bank of the Po. As a matter of fact, however, the enemy had by now already prepared to evacuate the Duchies; Ancona was given up, the garrisons of Pavia and Piacenza were withdrawn early in June, and on the 12th the troops at Bologna fell back upon Ferrara, preparatory to retiring across the Po. The Duchess of Parma now fled to Switzerland, while the Duke of Modena joined the staff of the Emperor Franz Josef.

On June 12 the 5th Corps commenced its march to the north, passed the Apennines, by bad roads and in tempestuous weather, about the 16th, and by the 27th Uhrich's division was concentrated in Parma. It was not, however, until the end of the month that the 5th Corps was ultimately reunited at Piadena.

No forward movement was made by the Allies either on the 9th or 10th, and the time was passed by the troops in the rest they so much needed, and by the Emperor Napoleon in perfecting his arrangements for the advance. To reach the Mincio from the Ticino, it was necessary to cross all the northern tributaries of the Po—each of which—the Adda, the Serio, the Oglio, the Mella and the Chiese—forms an excellent defensive line for an army retreating eastward.

It was not yet definitely known to what extent the Austrians had really suffered at Magenta, and it was confidently expected that Gyulai would stand on the Adda, whose torrent can only be passed at the bridges of Vaprio and Cassano, Lodi and Pizzighettone. The roads which lead across the river at the two latter places are that from Milan to Crema by Melegnano and that from Pavia to Mantua, and it was only by these roads that the Second Army was conducting its retreat. It was known, too, that the bulk of the army was about Lodi, and it was presumed that Gyulai would await attack on the lower portion of the Adda.

Reconnaissances sent along the Lodi road soon made it clear that the town was evacuated and that the Austrians—abandoning all attempt to defend the line of the river—were in full retreat, and the Emperor Napoleon then resolved to follow by the northern road, crossing the Adda at Vaprio and Cassano. Vaprio was given up to the troops under Victor Emmanuel and Garibaldi, while the bulk of the French corps prepared to cross at Cassano.

In pursuance of these intentions it was necessary first to recall the 1st, 2nd, and 4th Corps to the Milan—Cassano line. On the 11th the 1st Corps was directed on Linate and Limito, MacMahon moved on Paullo and Gavazzo, while Niel took, in Milan, the place of Canrobert who marched to Melzo.

The Italian Army, starting on the 10th, reached Monza on that day and Vimercate on the 11th, intending to reach the Adda on the day following.

Canrobert reached Cassano on the 12th, but the four bridges—road and railway—over the Muzza canal and the Adda, had been destroyed by the troops of the enemy retiring from Milan, and three pontoon and other bridges had to be thrown across; this work was completed long before dark and the 3rd Corps, crossing over, reached Treviglio that night. The 1st Corps occupied Melzo, Pozzuolo and Vignate, the 2nd Albignano and Truccazzano; the 5th Corps bivouacked at Pioltello, while the Guard was at Gorgonzola. The Italians, crossing the Adda at Vaprio, had occupied Ciserano, Cologno, Lurano, Pagazzano, Morengo and Romano—thus covering the front and left of the 3rd Corps.

On the 13th MacMahon moved over to the left bank and reached Caravaggio; the 1st Corps marched to Treviglio, which Canrobert vacated, moving to Mozzanica; while in rear Niel with the 4th Corps reached Albignano, Trecella and Pozzuolo, and the Guard Le Fornaci—both these last ready to cross next day. On the 14th the Guard, with the Imperial Headquarters, marched to Treviglio; the 3rd Corps crossed the Serio at Mozzanica and pursued, from Antignate, the Soncino road, leaving the Calcio road free for the 2nd Corps following in rear. The 1st Corps moved up to Mozzanica, while the 4th marched to Caravaggio. Thus the French Army had its front on the Oglio covered by the 2nd and 3rd Corps at Urago and Soncino, while the Guard, the 1st and the 4th Corps were massed a short distance in rear. On this day the Italian divisions on the left reached Coccaglio and Castegnate, thus threatening the Austrian right and extending a hand to Garibaldi.

Any intention which Gyulai might have entertained on the 8th of striking at the flank of his enemy was definitely abandoned on the full results of the action at Melegnano becoming known, and late that night orders for the continuance of the retreat were issued as under:—

The 1st Corps to move from Borghetto on Bertonico, cross the Adda and take up a position beyond Gombito.
The 2nd Corps—also from Borghetto—to move north and hold as long as possible the passages over the Muzza on the Borghetto—Lodi and Lodi—Castelpuste Orlengo roads—eventually retiring on the last named place.

The 5th Corps to move to Castelpuste Orlengo.

The 3rd Corps to form a reserve to the 2nd Corps behind the Muzza, retiring eventually on Castelpuste Orlengo.

The 5th and 9th Corps were each to give a battalion for the strengthening of the Piacenza garrison, and Urban was directed to abandon the projected expedition to the Valtelin and to retire from Canonica, Romana, Urago and Bagnolo to Montechiaro. It was found, however, to be impossible to carry out the above orders in their entirety, and consequently the movements on the 9th were unimportant.

It was now ordered that the strong places Piacenza, Pizzighettone and Cremona were to be evacuated, and their fortifications, as far as possible, dismantled, and it was calculated that the garrisons thus set free, from those and similar places, would add some 14,000 men to the effectives of the Second Army.

To effect the required concentration on the Chiese the following orders were issued on the 9th:—

The 7th Corps to move on the 10th by Crema, Orzinovi, Leno to Montechiaro—arriving on the 14th.

The 8th, with Mensdorff's Cavalry Division, to move on the 11th by Crema, Orzinovi, Manerbio to Montechiaro—arriving on the 14th.

The 1st to move on the 10th by Soresina, Castel Visconti, and Mottella to Carpenedolo—arriving on the 13th.

The 2nd to move on the 10th by Soresina, Castel Visconti and Gabbiano to Carpenedolo—arriving on the 13th.

The 3rd to move on the 10th by Soresina and Acqualunga to Carpenedolo—arriving on the 14th.

The 5th to move on the 10th by Zanengo, Farfengo, Quinzano and Pralboino to Casalmore—arriving on the 14th.

Urban to move on the 12th by Urago d'Oglio, Conticelle to Castenedolo—arriving on the 14th.

The 9th Corps to reach Acquanegra (west of Cremona),

on the 10th, and to move thence by Cigognolo, Piadena and Marcaria to Piubega—arriving on the 14th.

Army Headquarters to move on the 10th by Soresina and Verolanova to Carpenedolo—arriving on the 14th.

In issuing the above, Gyulai expressed his intention, if the enemy did not harass the retreat, of concentrating the whole of the Second Army in the Lonato—Castiglione position.

Late on the evening of this day Benedek represented that for the 7th and 8th Corps to hold the passages of the Adda until the 11th would, from the proximity of the Allies, probably bring on an action, and sanction was therefore accorded to his proposal to evacuate his position during the night of the 9th-10th; but he was enjoined to burn the bridges behind him and to remain with both corps on the left bank during the 10th. The 3rd Corps was at the same time ordered to move to the left bank and to destroy the bridges after crossing.

The march orders for the 10th were carried out with some slight alterations; the Cavalry Division which was to have marched on the 11th withdrew from Lodi on the 10th and reached Crema. The 1st Corps bivouacked at Azzanello instead of at Castel Visconti.

The garrison of Piacenza—some nine battalions of infantry, one and three-quarter squadrons, two batteries, one company of garrison artillery and two of engineers, under Major-General Roesgen—quitted the fortress at 2 p.m. The commander had been ordered to join the army by way of Brescello and Borgoforte; but a revolt had broken out in Parma, the town of Fiorenzola was already in the hands of the revolutionary party, and Roesgen wisely decided on retreating by Pizzighettone and the left bank of the Po, and was able to join the 5th Corps the same night. Of the guns in the fortress, 91 were sent by water to Borgoforte, five by land to Mantua, while about 130 others were destroyed or spiked; the two outer forts were blown up, and one pier and two arches of the Trebbia bridge were destroyed.

The commandant of Brescia was directed to stand fast, if possible, until the 11th, when he was to retire with the garrison to

Lonato, after sending all the railway rolling stock to Verona and blowing up the two bridges on the Chiese at Ponte San Marco.

On the 11th the moves were carried out as previously arranged, with the exception that the 3rd Corps this day reached Padernello beyond Acqualunga, while Urban, who was not to have retired before the 12th, but whose position at Vaprio—Canonica had been somewhat threatened, fell back—one brigade by Cologno—Romano, the other by Morengo; but the Serio being in flood, the only bridge available was that at Mozzanica and the crossing was greatly delayed, with the result that the brigades only reached Antignate, Romano and Fara. On this day, too, Montenuovo's division fell back behind the Serio and held an outpost line on that river from Crema to Sola.

On the 11th three more strong places were evacuated by the Austrians. Early in the afternoon the heavy guns of Pizzighettone were either destroyed or sent off to Mantua; the bridge over the Adda was set on fire and the garrison withdrew. In the same way Cremona was evacuated, the guns being removed to Mantua; while Brescia was also denuded of troops and munitions, the bridges over the Chiese being blown up as soon as the garrison had crossed at Ponte San Marco.

The retirement of the Austrians on the 12th was carried out without any interference from the Allies, and, so far as the Austrian information went, none of the enemy's regular troops had passed the Adda up to midday, although some of Garibaldi's men had been seen in the neighbourhood of Coccaglio. Urban had this day reached Chiari and Cizzago, and had sent a small force of all arms towards Pontoglio to watch the crossing there and patrol towards Palazzolo. This detachment at once reported that Palazzolo had been occupied in force since the previous day, that reinforcements had arrived there during the night—of which 4,000 men had pushed on to Brescia—and further that Garibaldi was advancing on Pontoglio.

The somewhat premature evacuation of Brescia had left Urban in a critical position, since his right and rear were both threatened by Garibaldi's troops. He was accordingly ordered to fall back as rapidly as possible behind the Mella, while Reznicek's brigade was directed to move on the evening of the 12th to Azzano-Capriano, secure the crossing at that spot and push strong patrols towards Brescia.

News coming in to Army Headquarters this evening that Brescia had been occupied by 12,000 Italians under Garibaldi and Cialdini, decided Gyulai to effect some alterations in his dispositions for the 13th: the 7th Corps marched to Castenedolo, the 8th to Offlaga and Cignano, Mensdorff to Faverzano, the 3rd Corps stood fast at Padernello, the 2nd at Quinzano and the 5th at Verolanova and Pontevico, while the 9th Corps marched to Marcaria and Bozzolo, Reznicek had pushed forward very early on the roads leading to Brescia, maintaining communication in rear with the 7th Corps, but on Urban crossing the Mella and establishing himself in Poncarale, Bagnolo and Capriano, Reznicek fell back upon the 1st Corps.

On the 14th the Austrians occupied the following places:—

Urban in Castenedolo.
The 1st Corps in Bagnolo.
The 7th at Montechiaro with a brigade in Calcinato.
The 8th and Cavalry Division in Leno.
The 5th in Gottolengo and Isorella.
The 3rd in Gambara.
The 2nd in Pralboino.
The 9th in Marcaria.

On the 15th MacMahon crossed the Oglio at Calcio and took up a position in front of Urago, the Imperial Guard and 3rd Corps closing up to him in rear and forming a second line at Romano, Covo and Fontanella; the remainder of the French corps did not move, but the Italians reached Brescia, with Garibaldi's troops in their front moving towards the Chiese.

During Urban's occupation of Vaprio—Canonica, Garibaldi had been at Bergamo, hesitating to advance further without support, but learning on the 12th that Vaprio had been vacated, he pushed forward by Martinengo and Palazzolo, crossed the

Oglio and, as has been already stated, entered Brescia on the morning of the 13th. Next day, finding that the head of the Italian divisions in rear were in touch with him, he advanced to San Eufemia, where it was evident that he must, ere long, become engaged with Urban's troops. These were disposed as follows: one brigade (Eckert, formerly Schaffgotsche) in Castenedolo with outposts towards Brescia, Gintowt's brigade more to the east on the Montechiaro road with the reserve artillery, with Rupprecht to the north watching Ciliverghe and Rezzato.

Late that night Garibaldi was ordered by the King to advance on the 15th towards Lonato and to repair the bridge at Bettoletto, for which operation he was promised the support of Sambuy's cavalry. Garibaldi prepared to carry out these instructions, but having learnt in the morning that Urban was in Castenedolo, it was necessary to guard against any attack on the right flank. Counting on the speedy arrival of the promised cavalry, Garibaldi sent the whole of his 1st Regiment to contain Rupprecht, occupied Bettola and Ciliverghe with a battalion of the 2nd, and moved himself with the rest of his force towards Bettoletto.

In the orders for the 15th which had been sent to Urban, he had been directed to stand fast at Castenedolo until 11 a.m., at which hour it was arranged that the 1st Corps would cross the Chiese. Urban had made all his arrangements for withdrawal accordingly, but before he had marched off he was attacked by Garibaldi's troops. The skirmishers of the 1st Regiment of the Cacciatori delle Alpi came upon Rupprecht's advanced troops between 7.30 and 8 a.m. and drove them in, but reinforcements coming up the Italians in their turn were forced back to the line of the railway. Fearing now that his retreat might be threatened from the direction of Ciliverghe, Urban sent thither one battalion, two guns and a squadron of cavalry, and these engaging the single battalion of Garibaldi's 2nd Regiment threw it back in some disorder.

In the meantime Cialdini had been hurried forward with the 4th Italian Division and reached San Eufemia just as the action came to a close, Urban wisely deciding, under all the circumstances, not to press the slight temporary advantage he had gained. He accordingly broke off the action about 3 p.m. and fell back upon Calcinato. Cialdini bivouacked at Rezzato and San Eufemia and Garibaldi about Bettoletto.

Neither side experienced much loss in this affair, the Austrians having twelve killed, 89 wounded and missing; while the Italians lost fifteen killed, 120 wounded and had 73 men taken prisoners.

While the above action was in progress, the 1st Austrian Corps had reached Chiarini, but as the brigades were preparing to bivouac, a report arrived from Urban of the attack made upon him and of the consequent threatened turning of the Austrian right. Clam thereupon sent two of his brigades towards Calcinato and another to Vighizzolo, but finding Urban's retreat was unmolested these brigades returned to Chiarini. The Cavalry Division moved to Rho, the 8th Corps to Montechiaro, the 5th to Carpenedolo, the 3rd to Castel Goffredo, the 2nd to San Cassiano, the 9th to Gazzoldo, and Army Headquarters to Castiglione delle Stiviere.

After eleven days of retreat the Second Army was now established in an admirable position behind the Chiese, ready again to offer battle to the Allies. The deliberation, too, with which the retirement had been conducted, had allowed time for the Austrian military authorities to initiate, and to some extent to carry through, arrangements for increasing and reorganising the Austrian forces; and the opportunity may perhaps here well be taken of describing, as briefly as possible, the general scheme of reorganisation, whereby it was hoped that success—which now for so many weeks had eluded the army—might yet be attracted to its banners.

On May 26 an Imperial rescript had emanated from Vienna, directing the calling out of the First Army, and stating that the Emperor Franz Josef himself would proceed to Italy and there assume the command-in-chief of both armies, so soon as the First should be ready to take the field; until then the force already in Italy, as well as all details *en route* thither, were to remain as heretofore under Gyulai's command. Feldzeugmeister Count Wimpffen was placed at the head of the First Army, while the commands of the Third and Fourth Armies, intended for the defence of the Austrian frontiers, were confided respectively to Prince Liechtenstein and Count Schlick.

On May 30 the Emperor himself proceeded to Verona, accompanied by the Imperial Headquarters Staff, and while exercising a general supervision over the operations, for the actual conduct of which Gyulai was apparently still in the main responsible, he occupied himself principally in the perfecting of the arrangements for the increase and reorganisation of the Austrian forces already in the field or approaching thereto. A statement of the composition of the different armies as newly organised will be found in the appendices, but it may be convenient to state here that the First Army was to consist of the 2nd, 3rd, 9th, 10th, and 11th Corps and the Cavalry Division of General Zedtwitz, while the Second Army contained the 1st, 5th, 7th, and 8th, with the Cavalry Division under Mensdorff.

On June 16 the Emperor Franz Josef took over the command of the Second Army, so as to bring its movements into line with those of the First Army, which had by this time arrived in the theatre of war. Gyulai's idea of making a stand on the Chiese was now no longer entertained and he received orders to move on this day towards the Mincio, in readiness to cross to the left bank on the 17th and take up the positions which had been assigned to the corps under his command.

To cover the retirement of the Second Army, Urban was directed to establish himself on the 16th between Lonato and Castiglione, following the rear of the army, partly by Peschiera, partly by Volta and Valeggio. On the 18th it was intended that Urban's division should be broken up, Rupprecht's brigade going to strengthen the garrison of Verona, while the others were to be distributed among the various corps of the reconstituted armies.

The following movements were to commence on the 17th:—

The 7th and 8th Corps to move between Peschiera and Valeggio and to be jointly responsible for that portion of the line of the Mincio.

The 1st Corps to Somma compagna to form a reserve

The 2nd Corps to march to Mantua there to be incorporated in the First Army.

The 3rd Corps to Quaderni and to watch the line of the river from Valeggio to Pozzolo.

The 5th Corps to Villafranca to form a reserve.

The 9th Corps to march to Mozzecane and join the First Army, linking on to the outpost line of the 3rd and carrying it on to just above Goito.

The Headquarters of the Second Army to move to Custoza.

FIRST ARMY.

The 11th Corps to march from Mantua to Tormene and establish outposts about Goito—joining those of the 9th Corps. The Cavalry Division of Zedtwitz to move to about San Zenone. The Headquarters of the First Army to Mozzecane.

Garrisons for Mantua and Legnago were to be found by the 2nd Corps, while the 1st provided those of Peschiera and Verona.

In accordance with the foregoing, Gyulai directed that on the 16th the 7th Corps should march to Desenzano, the 8th Corps and the Cavalry Division to Guidizzolo, the 1st to Peschiera, the 3rd to Goito, and the 5th to Volta, while Urban moved to Lonato and Castiglione.

From reports which had reached Gyulai on the night of the 15th, it appeared that the Allies were standing fast in front, while an outflanking movement on a large scale was in course of execution, and that it was intended to move large forces by Lake Garda to operate on the north of the Mincio position. The Imperial Headquarters thereupon decided that the retreat of the

Second Army—then already commenced—should be counter-manded and that Gyulai should reoccupy the Lonato—Castiglione position with a view to striking a decisive blow at the Allies before the 5th Corps, under Prince Napoleon, could join them from the south.

In accordance with this determination the 7th Corps was ordered to move to Lonato extending its right to the lake, the 8th Corps to Castiglione, the 1st to Castel Venzago as a reserve (with the Cavalry Division at Guidizzolo) to the 7th and 8th Corps.

Urban was to join the 8th Corps, and Gyulai's Headquarters was to be at Pozzolengo. These positions were to be maintained during the 17th and the 1st Corps and Urban's troops were to be hurled against the enemy's flank; in the event of the Allies being driven back to the Chiese, the crossings at Ponte San Marco and at Montechiaro were to be once more held. Should the positions of the 7th and 8th Corps be attacked in force, the 3rd Corps from Goito and the 5th from Volta were to be used, as seemed best, either to strike at the enemy's flank or to strengthen the Lonato—Castiglione position.

The 6th Corps, then in Tyrol, was to endeavour to threaten the enemy's flank from the Upper Chiese valley, moving by Storo on Vestone and Salo; the commander was advised that the army would probably move forward towards Brescia on the 21st, and he was particularly enjoined to concentrate in as great strength as possible about Vestone on the 20th.

These counter-orders were evidently quite unexpected, and some of the units of the Second Army had already covered some considerable distance in their retreat to the Mincio before the fresh orders overtook them. It was then impossible for the directions to be complied with in full that day, and it was not until the 17th that Gyulai was able to report that the Lonato—Castiglione position had been reoccupied as directed.

On this day the First Army was in position behind the Mincio—the 9th Corps between Roverbella and Belvidere, the 2nd in and south of Mantua, the 10th to the east of Mantua, the 11th in reserve about Tormene; the Cavalry Division was on its way to Verona, and Army Headquarters was at Mozzecane.

The Commander of the 7th Corps now asked for another division to strengthen his right, and Urban was ordered to move on the 18th to Desenzano, pushing one brigade to Padenghe and stationing another on the northern side of Desenzano. Gyulai particularly asked sanction to concentrate his troops for the purpose of more effectual support, pointing out that Lonato—the key of the position—was held by the 7th Corps, which had recently, from various causes, been greatly reduced in numbers, and that the distance at which the 1st Corps was posted effectually prevented anything like timely support.

To this a reply was given that there was no intention of really holding the position, which would only be maintained so long as the enemy made no serious attack upon it. Gyulai was also informed that the army would probably be withdrawn behind the Mincio on the 20th, and the orders issued to the 6th Corps in Tyrol were now cancelled.

On this day, the 18th, Urban's division, now commanded by Rupprecht, made the moves ordered on the previous day, while the other units of the Second Army remained halted. Early in the afternoon, however, orders were issued that the withdrawal of the Second Army behind the Mincio was to be so carried out that all the units should have crossed and reached their allotted positions by midday on the 21st, the 3rd Corps to Pozzolo, the 5th to Valeggio, the 8th to Prentina and Salionze, the 1st, 7th, and Cavalry to Quaderni, Mozzecane and Malvicina in reserve.

On the 18th Count Gyulai tendered the resignation of his command and his place was filled by Count Schlick, lately commanding the Fourth Army.

On the 20th and 21st the retreat was resumed; a large number of crossings had been prepared over the Mincio, *viz*:—

Two bridges at Peschiera;
One bridge ,, Salionze;
One ,, ,, Monzambano;
One ,, ,, Valeggio;

One „ „ Pozzolo;
Three bridges „ Goito;

And by the latter date both armies were in position on the left bank from Peschiera to Mantua, having, to all appearance, no other intention than to dispute with the enemy the passage of the river.

The 10th Corps, drawn well back behind the left, covered that flank from any attack from the right bank of the Po.

In the meantime the Allies had resumed their measured advance after the action at Castenedolo; on the 16th the 1st, 2nd, and 3rd Corps, with part of the Guard, crossed the Oglio, when the most advanced points occupied by the French were Chiari, Castrezzato, Comezzano and Orzinovi. The rest of the army was on or behind the Oglio. The Emperor was at Calcio, while the King was at Castegnate with his divisions in and about Brescia, On the 17th the Italians advanced in two columns, the 1st and 2nd Divisions by the Castenedolo road, the 3rd and 4th towards Rezzato. The French arrived on the Mella and pushed Desvaux's cavalry on to Bagnolo and Montirone, and the next day the Emperor reached the right bank of the Chiese; the marching was slow but the heat was extreme.

The French were now disposed in order of battle: Baraguey d' Hilliers was on the left moving on Lonato and Castiglione, MacMahon in the centre at San Zeno and Borgo Satollo, and Niel on the right at Bagnolo; in the rear was the Guard at Brescia with Canrobert at Poncarale.

The army halted on the 19th and 20th, and received a cavalry reinforcement in the shape of a brigade of cavalry of the Guard under General Morris.

Reconnaissances sent out on the 19th found that Montechiaro was occupied, but on the morrow it became known that the position had been completely abandoned. Moving forward again on the 21st the 4th Corps crossed the Chiese at Mezzane and occupied Carpenedolo with the flanks covered by the cavalry under Partouneaux and Desvaux; the 3rd Corps closed up in rear of the 4th, remaining, however, on the right bank; while the 2nd Corps occupied Montechiaro, with the 1st behind the river at Rho. Of the Piedmontese one division (3rd) was at Desenzano, with the 1st and 5th in support at Lonato. Victor Emmanuel held his 2nd Division in reserve with his Headquarters at Calcinato, while the Imperial Headquarters was with the Guard at Castenedolo. On the 22nd MacMahon again moved on, occupying Castiglione, while the Guard crossed to Montechiaro.

No forward movement was made on the 23rd, but reconnaissances were sent out to cover thoroughly the whole country between the Chiese and the Mincio; while from the hills about Castiglione the brothers Goddard repeated a balloon ascent which they had made two days before from Castenedolo. From all available sources of information it seemed clear that there was considerable movement among the Austrians; that Solferino, Cavriana, Guidizzolo and Medole were occupied, and that heavy columns were about Goito and Pozzolengo. To the Emperor all this seemed merely to prove that the Austrians—anxious to discover the points where the passage of the Mincio was likely to be attempted—were supporting, in considerable strength, the troops which they had thrown forward to gain information; and the Emperor Napoleon can hardly be blamed if it failed to occur to him that the Austrians—having evacuated the strong positions on the Chiese and permitted their occupation by the Allies—should now be about to offer battle with the Mincio at their backs and in a position far inferior to that which they had voluntarily given up.

It was, however, the unexpected which was about to happen, and which was to result in the greatest battle, in point of numbers, which had, up to then, been fought since Leipzic.

Moltke has discussed the question whether Piacenza should have been evacuated, or whether, as some have held, it should have been made use of as a strong flank position, whence Lombardy might have been successfully defended. A retreat behind the Po would have put an end to all pursuit, while the 10th and 11th Corps might have joined the army by way of Mantua and

Borgoforte. Had the Allies then still held on their way to the Mincio, the Austrians could have moved on their right flank from or below Piacenza, or could even have returned to the right bank of the Ticino and cut the communications in rear of the French and Italian armies.

Against all this must be said that, since the Austrians were not pursued, they were in no immediate need of the protection of the fortress, and that flank movements when executed from beyond a certain distance lose much of their value. A position on the flank behind the canal must have checked the march of the Allies on Milan; whereas one behind the Po would have had no effect on their onward movement. By holding fast at Piacenza, the Austrians were not drawing nearer to their reinforcements, while they were allowing the enemy time to strengthen his hold on Lombardy. Moltke considers that the evacuation of Piacenza was justified, since its fortifications were not sufficiently completed for it to stand alone; but none the less a bad impression was made by its enforced abandonment.

There is very much to be said in favour of a stand on the Chiese, as Gyulai had intended. The left bank everywhere commanded the right, the northern flank of the position could not be turned, while if the left flank were attempted, there was there admirable ground for the employment of the Austrian cavalry in support of the main army attacking across the river. At the worst the fortresses of the Quadrilateral were only one day's march in rear, and if the hilly country behind the Chiese increased the difficulties of retreat, it added, at least in equal measure, to those attending an advance.

CHAPTER 9

The Battle of Solferino

In order to discover something definite about the dispositions of the Franco-Italian Army, and also to regain touch, which had been temporarily relaxed, the commander of the Second Army sent out on the night of the 21st a strong patrol, consisting of two squadrons of cavalry and two horse-artillery guns, under Major von Appel of the 12th Uhlans. This patrol was ordered to cross the Mincio at Monzambano and make for Pozzolengo, move next day by Rivoltella to Lonato, and return by way of Castiglione, Guidizzolo and Volta to Valeggio.

Major von Appel was not, however, able completely to fulfil all that had been confided to him; he came everywhere upon the enemy in considerable force, and was never able to pierce the screen behind which their main strength was concealed. But from the reports which this officer sent in during his tour, rather than perhaps from the general conclusions to be drawn from his expedition as a whole, the Imperial Headquarter Staff came to the conclusion that only 'part of the Allied Army was on the left bank of the Chiese—*viz*, the Italians to the north in the neighbourhood of the Lake of Garda by Desenzano and Lonato, and some of the French troops in the hilly country about Esenta, Castiglione and Carpenedolo.

With the retirement of the Austrians behind the Mincio, the Emperor Franz Josef and his military advisers had apparently by no means relinquished all idea of a return to the offensive; the numerous bridges which had been constructed, or which were already in existence, over the river had all been retained; many commanding positions on the right bank had been occupied and entrenched, and from these and other signs and preparations, it seems tolerably clear that the Austrians were only awaiting an opportunity, following upon the concentration of their armies, once again to endeavour to fall upon and overwhelm the enemy.

The whole force under the Emperor Franz Josef was now indeed strengthened and recuperated, and its concentration effected, and it was resolved to assume the offensive while the enemy was engaged in the passage of the Chiese, and before the 60,000 men—said to be threading the passes of the Apennines—could strike at the lower reaches of the Po and turn the Austrian left flank. Late then on the 22nd, after the return of the Emperor to Villafranca from an inspection of the position of the 1st Corps at Quaderni, orders were sent out directing the advance of the armies across the Mincio on the 24th. Before, however, these orders had much more than started on their way to the corps concerned, the date of the intended movement was changed, in the hope of falling upon the Allies before their passage of the Chiese had been completed.

The Army Order detailing the proposed movement is too long to quote *verbatim*, but the following comprises its main points:

> The Imperial Army will resume the offensive on the 24th, and the operations, wherein both armies will be engaged, will consist in—(1) Crossing the Mincio; (2) the overthrow of the enemy in the immediate neighbourhood; (3) the advance to the Chiese; (4) the preliminaries to an action on the Chiese should the enemy there concentrate.
>
> Movements of the Second Army.
>
> The 8th Corps will cross at Salionze, being previously joined in Peschiera by a brigade of the 6th Corps (Major-General Reichlin-Meldegg[1]), and will move on Pozzo-

---

1. This brigade actually joined during the night of the 22nd-23rd.

lengo.

The 5th Corps will cross at Valeggio and move on Solferino.

The 1st Corps will cross at Valeggio in rear of the 5th, and will move on Volta and Cavriana.

Mensdorff's Cavalry Division, and in its rear the 7th Corps, will cross at Ferri after the 3rd Corps, and will move, the Cavalry to the east of Cavriana, the 7th Corps to Foresto.

Movements of the First Army.

This army, as the left flank, will at first remain refused and will protect Goito from any possible attack. As soon as the movement of the Second Army has developed, the 3rd Corps will cross at Ferri, moving on Guidizzolo.

The 9th Corps will cross at Goito and also move on Guidizzolo.

In rear of the 9th Corps will cross Zedtwitz's Cavalry Division and then the 11th Corps, which will move to the west of Cereta. The Cavalry Division will protect the left flank towards Medole with detachments pushed forward to Casaloldo and Castel Goffredo.

The 2nd Corps will detach two brigades to the 9th Corps and these will move to Marcaria to protect the left.

The passage of the river to begin at 9 a.m. with the Second Army, and at 10 a.m. with the First.

In the event of a reverse both armies will retire in the same manner and reoccupy their original positions behind the Mincio.

On the 24th the Imperial Headquarters will be at Valeggio.

Movements for the 25th: Second Army.

The 8th Corps and Reichlin's brigade to Lonato and Desenzano.

The 5th Corps to Esenta.

The 1st Corps to Castiglione delle Stiviere.

The 7th Corps to Le Fontane.

Mensdorff's Cavalry Division, supported by the 5th Corps to Montechiaro.

First Army.

The 9th Corps to between Carpenedolo and Acqua Fredda.

The 3rd and 11th Corps to Carpenedolo and San Vigilio.

Zedtwitz's Cavalry Division to Acqua Fredda and Casalmoro.

Of the two brigades of the 2nd Corps one to move to Acquanegra and one to Asola.

Movements to commence at 9 a.m. Imperial Headquarters at Guidizzolo.

Then follows the after-order, directing that the crossing on the 24th be now carried out on the 23rd, and that the forward movement detailed for the 25th should now be commenced on the 24th.

The officer commanding the 6th Corps in Tyrol was also enjoined to conform to the movements above indicated by marching towards Salo and Gavardo, and the Commandant of Mantua was ordered to prepare a bridge and bridge-head at Borgoforte. From a consideration of all the above, one is led to the conclusion that the offensive was resumed on the presumption that on June 23, at least a considerable portion of the Allied Army had yet to cross the Chiese, and that what had already passed over was little more than strong advanced guards. The Austrian mainstroke then was to be directed upon Castiglione and the three passages of the Chiese at Ponte San Marco, Montechiaro, and Carpenedolo; for this purpose two corps (5th and 1st) were to advance on Solferino and Cavriana along the Castiglione road; two other corps (9th and 3rd) with the same objective to Guidizzolo; Mensdorff was to maintain connexion between the two armies; two corps (7th and 11th) were to be held in reserve at Foresto and Cereta; while the flanks were to be covered by the 8th Corps at Pozzolengo and by Zedtwitz and part of the 2nd Corps between Medole and Marcaria.

By the evening of the 23rd the passage of the Mincio and the onward march of the Austrian corps to their destinations were completed in accordance with the orders which had been issued.

On this date the Austrians were able to count upon the following numbers:—

With the Second Army: the 1st (including Reichlin's brigade), 5th, 7th and 8th Corps and Mensdorff's Cavalry Division numbered 102 battalions, 36 squadrons and 49 batteries—a total of 86,273 men, 11,023 horses and 392 guns.

With the First Army: the 2nd, 3rd, 9th, 10th, and 11th Corps and Zedtwitz's Cavalry Division com- prised 121½ battalions, 52 squadrons and 45 batteries—a total of 103,375 men, 11,608 horses and 360 guns, or a grand total for both armies of 189,648 men, 22,631 horses and 752 guns.

The Allies acknowledge to the following numbers:—

With the French—including the 5th Corps but exclusive of some 8,900 cavalry and infantry with General Ulloa— there were 198 battalions, 80 squadrons and 432 guns, or 118,019 men and 10,206 horses.

With the Italians there were 96 battalions, 37 squadrons and 90 guns or 55,584 men and 4,147 horses, making a grand total of 173,603 men, 14,353 horses and 522 guns.

It is now necessary to give some description of the ground over which this great battle was about to be fought.

The Mincio, issuing from the Lago di Garda, runs due south, while the direction of the hills on both banks runs at right angles almost towards it; those on the right bank, with which alone we have to do hero, coming down from the north and northwest, strike the Mincio in a south-easterly direction. The hilly country on the right bank of the Mincio, thus forms a tolerably regular parallelogram from northwest to southeast, the four angles of which are Lonato, Peschiera, Volta and Castiglione. This parallelogram of hills is about twelve miles in length and eight in width, and is divided longitudinally by the Redone, a little stream coming out of the hills between Lonato and Castiglione and running into the Mincio.

The hills rise gradually from the shores of the lake in successive irregular wave lines, the last towards the plain towering high above the rest, and forming, as it were, a mighty wall round the west and south sides of the parallelogram. The south side, above all, is remarkable for its height and steepness all along its length from Castiglione to Volta. Being formed of a succession of long steep ridges, strongly indentated, it looks from the plain like the ruins of some Titanic stronghold, destroyed by time and overgrown with grass. Two points, higher than the rest, stand in the centre of this line of ridges. These two points are Solferino and Cavriana. Both detached from the others, and sloping down precipitously towards the plain, they resemble two bastions, while the lower, but scarcely less precipitous, slopes of San Cassiano between them may well represent the curtain of these gigantic bastions.

From the interior another range of hills runs down towards the outer one. It skirts the north or left bank of the little stream Redone, and comes down with it from the neighbourhood of Lonato, in an almost southerly direction, to within a mile from the heights of Solferino. It there makes a sudden bend to the north- east, runs on for a couple of miles in this direction, and then breaks off.

At the point where it breaks off lies Pozzolengo, and at the point where the ridge approaches nearest to Solferino, stands in an isolated position the church of Madonna delia Scoperta. Solferino and Cavriana on the outer ridge and Pozzolengo and Madonna della Scoperta on the inner, mark the position of the Austrians in the Mincio hills. The relative positions of these four points is such that if a line were drawn round them, it would give the figure of a truncated cone; Cavriana and Pozzolengo forming the base of it towards the Mincio, and Solferino and Madonna della Scoperta the top towards Castiglione and Lonato.

With the exception of the road near the lake to Peschiera, the others leading through this hilly country to the Mincio all touch one or more of these points; consequently their possession shuts the hills of the Mincio to an advancing army.

While they thus in their ensemble give the command of the Mincio hills, each of these four points forms the centre of a group of ridges branching out from that centre. The position of the Austrians in the hills must thus be represented as a colossal natural redoubt with four bastions, each of them with numerous outworks and only assailable at the angles.

From whichever side the traveller approaches the Mincio hills, one of the first objects which will attract his attention is a square, weather-beaten tower on a high conical hill covered with green turf. It is the *Spia d'Italia*, so called because from it the eye can pry over a large part of the Lombard plain, over the shores of the Lago di Garda, and over the Mincio far beyond the spires and domes of Mantua. The hill on which it is built, called the Bocca di Solferino, rises abruptly to the northwest of the village to which it has given its name.

After attaining two-thirds of its height, it throws out two spurs like two horns, one to its left—sharp, narrow, precipitous, showing a bold outline towards the plain and falling off suddenly. It is called Monte di Cipressi, from a row of these trees which crown its summit conspicuous from afar. The other to the right, having no particular name, but commonly called Monte della Chiesa with the church of St. Nicholas on the top. Stretching out in the direction of Castiglione, it rises abruptly from the valley of the Redone, and throws out towards this river a lower, but equally abrupt, branch similarly crowned with a church—that of San Pietro. On the other side—that is towards the plain—it slopes down more gradually towards the Monte di Cipressi. In the hollow between the two lies the little hamlet of Pozzo di Solferino, as the villagers call it. The spurs, although forming part of the group of the Bocca, are separated by a depression in the ground from the Bocca itself, and this depression has been used to lead the roads from Castighone over the group to the village of Solferino behind it.

There are two of these roads—one which runs along the plain at the base of the hills and, leaving the village of Grole to its left, turns up between the Monte di Cipressi and the Monte della Chiesa to the hamlet of Pozzo di Solferino, and crosses the ridge between the Bocca di Solferino and the Monte della Chiesa; the other, leaving Castiglione and the outer ridge to its right, winds along the hills almost parallel to the former, and rising in a steep incline between Monte della Chiesa and the smaller spurs of San Pietro, tops the ridge at the same point as the road through the plain. Both roads united there run down to the village of Solferino.

Just where the two unite, rise the walls of the church of St. Nicholas, occupying the whole summit of the Bocca. These walls, about 20 to 30 feet high, enclose, besides the church, a belfry, the schools and the dwelling of the parish priest, which occupy three sides. In front of the church is a large open plot of ground, and to the right of it the hill, protected only by a low wall, descends abruptly towards the hill road which runs up to its foot. Beyond the walls of St. Nicholas the summit of the Bocca presents a narrow green plateau with another much whiter looking enclosure at its edge; this is the cemetery of Solferino.

Beyond the cemetery, but separated from it by a depression in the ground, begin the scale or ladders of Solferino, a succession of steep, precipitous ridges between the plain and the valley of the Redone, which extend as far as the little village of Grole.

The hill group of Solferino forms then a succession of formidable positions, easy to defend and very difficult to approach. In the two roads are deep and narrow defiles, flanked by the spurs between which they run up to the top of the ridge. By the ridge itself the advance is scarcely less dangerous, for each ridge is commanded by the following one. Besides this, each is likewise separated from the other by a strong depression in the ground, forming, as it were, the ditch to each of these successive positions.

While the position of Solferino is thus well protected in front and on the flanks, it is not less so in the rear; for, from the foot almost of the Bocca hill, rises another ridge sloping down terrace-like towards the scattered houses of the village of San Cassiano in the plain. Between this ridge and the base of the Bocca hill, the road from San Cassiano to the village of Solferino runs up. While the slopes of San Cassiano are held, it is, therefore, like the roads in front, a defile. The ridge of San Cassiano extends, in an almost uninterrupted line, to Cavriana, the sister group of Solferino, which had been chosen by the Austrians for their reserves.

Of a similar conformation as Solferino, the slopes of San Cassiano are to it what the scale are to Solferino—a kind of natural outwork. Both look down on what is called the Campo di Medole, an open plain devoid of trees, through which the main road from Castiglione passes to Goito. This road, coming out of Castiglione to the left of the Mincio hills, runs for about half a mile through a country like the rest of Upper Lombardy, covered with vineyards and mulberry trees, but less cut up by canals than other portions of it.

There being a scantiness of water, the vegetation is not very rich and the ground more open and adapted to military movements. After running through this country for a mile and a half, the road enters the Campo di Medole just at the point where a cross road, intersecting the plain, runs in a straight line to Medole. The main road continues for about two and a half miles in this open plain until it comes to the outskirts of the village of Guidizzolo, where the trees begin again. The open plain is scantily cultivated with only here and there a corn or a maize field and the rest bad pasture ground. About a mile from the southern outskirts of the Campo di Medole runs the road from Medole to Guidizzolo, and, parallel almost to the main road to Goito, another from Carpenedolo by Medole to Ceresara in the direction of Mantua.

In the orders given out overnight for the onward movements of the two armies on the 24th, Count Schlick had directed that the 8th Corps should move off at 8 a.m., the others at 9, while

Wimpffen ordered his 3rd and 9th Corps to march at 9, the cavalry at 10, and the others to conform to these movements

The Emperor Napoleon, on the other hand, in issuing his orders for the same day had directed that the following movements should commence not later than 3 a.m.:—

The 1st Corps from Esenta to Solferino.
The 2nd Corps from Castiglione to Cavriana.
The 3rd Corps from Mezzane to Medole.
The 4th Corps with the cavalry of Partouneaux and Desvaux—from Carpenedolo to Guidizzolo.
The Imperial Guard, with Headquarters, to Castiglione.
The Italian Army to move on to Pozzolengo, maintaining touch with the 1st Corps by means of the 2nd Division (Fanti), which had bivouacked north of Esenta.
The Austrians then on June 24 were to leave the line Pozzolengo—Solferino—Guidizzolo and gain the line Lonato—Castiglione—Carpenedolo; while the Allies were on the same date to abandon the positions Lonato—Castighone—Carpenedolo and move forward to the line Pozzolengo—Solferino—Guidizzolo. The result of such movements, executed the same day and on the same lines, could only be a general action, wherein the advantage must lie with that side which had taken the initiative. The Allies started from five to six hours earlier than their adversaries, and the latter were consequently taken greatly by surprise.

The events now about to be described may most conveniently be divided into three parts:—

1. The operations between Solferino and the lake of Garda—between the Piedmontese on the one side and the 8th and part of the 5th Austrian Corps on the other, *viz.* the operations in the north.
2. Those against Solferino and Cavriana—the 1st and 2nd French Corps and the Imperial Guard being pitted against the 5th, 7th and 1st Austrian Corps, *viz.* the operations in

the centre.

3. The battle in the plain, wherein Niel and Canrobert fought against the 3rd, 9th, and 11th Corps of the first Austrian Army, *viz.* the operations in the south.

The action commenced to the south; the 4th French Corps, on the right of the Allied Army, left its bivouac at 3 a.m., and its three divisions—de Luzy leading—took the road from Carpenedolo to Medole. De Luzy's front was covered by two squadrons of the 10th Chasseurs à Cheval, and these came upon some of the enemy's light cavalry rather more than two miles from Medole and drove them in, but their own further advance was arrested by the fire of the Austrians who had occupied the village with both infantry and artillery. Niel now ordered de Luzy to advance his division and carry Medole.

This important post had been occupied on the previous evening by two battalions of the Austrian 52nd Regiment, two guns and a few hussars belonging to Blumencron's brigade of Crenneville's division of the 9th Corps. Schaffgotsche had given orders for the march to be continued at 9 a.m. on the 24th, but as early as 5 that morning Crenneville reported that his outposts at Morino, to the northeast of Medole, had been attacked. Schaffgotsche then prepared to advance at once on Medole, but almost immediately the report was contradicted, and the corps commander, reluctant to move before his men had had their morning meal, decided to stand fast. At six o'clock, however, a report was received direct from the front stating that fighting had already for some considerable time been in progress at Medole and that the Austrians had been driven from the village.

The defenders of Medole had offered for something like three hours a very stubborn resistance to greatly superior numbers, attacking on two sides and supported by a powerful artillery. As soon as the attack developed, Major Urs, who commanded in Medole, sent word to his brigadier, Blumencron, then in camp to the west of Guidizzolo, but that commander, being himself unable to detect the sound of firing, decided to take no action whatever and did not even forward a report to his divisional chief. Driven at last from his defences on the west of the village, Urs defended Medole house by house, and when finally forced to fall back upon the remainder of the brigade, he was able only to bring off the equivalent of two companies with two officers—nine-tenths of the latter and four-fifths of the men being either killed, wounded or prisoners.

Lauingen's cavalry brigade had been formed up in rear of Medole—on the Ceresara side—to cover and support the retirement of the infantry, but Lauingen withdrew first half-way to Ceresara and, then, considering that the ground here was unsuitable for the movements of cavalry, he fell back behind Ceresara; finally retiring altogether and arriving at Goito about 9 a.m., and taking thenceforth no part or interest in the action. His divisional general, Zedtwitz, himself rode off in search of him, and the result of the action of these two cavalry commanders was the practical loss of the services of the mounted troops on the Austrian left flank for the rest of the day.

While the 4th Corps had been thus engaged at Medole the 3rd Corps, under Canrobert, starting at 2.30 a.m., crossed the Chiese opposite Visano and moved on Medole by Acqua Fredda and Castel Goffredo. This latter place was reached about 7, and being occupied only by a few mounted men was captured without difficulty, and Canrobert, now hearing the guns in action at Medole, ordered Renault's division to push on in that direction.

Part of Blumencron's brigade had also been in occupation of Casa Morino, and MacMahon, advancing early towards Cavriana from Castiglione, came upon this post and drove out its defenders; but seeing now that the 1st Corps on his left had been checked in its advance, MacMahon decided to content himself with holding his position for the present, in view of the large hostile columns now visible in the plain to his front. He suggested now to Niel that they should both take ground to their left—MacMahon for the purpose of drawing nearer to the 1st Corps and Niel to prevent any gap occurring between the 2nd and 4th. Niel, then engaged in front of Medole, promised to conform as soon as the village should be captured and Canrobert had drawn up to him on the right.

As a temporary measure, however, the cavalry under Partouneaux and Desvaux was ordered to occupy the interval between Niel and MacMahon. MacMahon then disposed his troops as follows: one of the brigades of the division of La Motterouge, deployed at right angles to the road, maintained touch between the 2nd Corps and Desvaux's cavalry, while the other remained in reserve behind the Casa Morino; Decaen's division formed to the left of La Motterouge in the direction of the 1st Corps.

The hostile columns noticed by the Duke of Magenta were the divisions of the 9th, 3rd, and 1st Corps advancing westwards. Schaffgotsche, however, seems even now to have been in ignorance of the fact that two complete French Corps were in his front, and still thought that Medole had been occupied by little more than the enemy's advanced troops, and that its recapture would scarcely delay the carrying out of the prescribed movement on Carpenedolo. The commander of the 9th Corps directed his 2nd Division (Crenneville) to march on Medole from its position to the east of Casa Morino, and of the three brigades of his 1st Division (Handl) he placed one on the Rebecco-Medole road, one still further south towards Ceresara, and the third in reserve, and arranged with Schwartzenberg that the 3rd Corps should move on Castiglione by way of Casa Morino. The country about here, however, being much broken and enclosed, the various brigades failed to keep touch, wandered apart and came independently into action. Crenneville moving on Medole was threatened on his right, was fired into on the left by Vinoy's division of the 4th Corps—which had been pushed well forward in the cultivation—and was unable to make any concerted attack.

Handl's brigades—widely separated at the outset—became more so as the advance was prosecuted and arrived independently before Medole, where the French had made careful preparations for their reception. At 9 a.m. the situation in this part of the field was as follows: what was left of Crenneville's two brigades stood on the main Mantua-Castiglione road and held a farm to the south of it and immediately north of Baite, confronting Vinoy's division of the 4th and the whole of the 2nd Corps; at Rebecco one of Handl's brigades was engaged with one of de Luzy's, while further south another was held in check by Le Noble, and Handl's third brigade, which had already suffered greatly in the action, had fallen back shattered to Guidizzolo, On the side of the French, de Failly's division of the 4th Corps supported de Luzy towards Rebecco and Baite.

The head of Canrobert's columns reached Medole shortly after nine o'clock, when the Commander was warned by Napoleon that an Austrian corps, of an estimated strength of 20,000 to 25,000 men, which had left Mantua on the 23rd, had its outposts at Acquanegra, but at the same time Canrobert was ordered to support Niel's right. Canrobert now pushed forward Jannin's brigade towards Ceresara.

In the centre Baraguey d'Hilliers had been ordered to march on the left of the 2nd Corps from Esenta to Solferino. His 2nd Division (Ladmirault) started the first at 3 o'clock and by 6 a.m. had arrived in front of the heights about Solferino, which were found to be held by the enemy. Ladmirault formed his division in three columns of attack—two to turn the flanks and the third to assault in front—and covered by the fire of the only four guns which had been able to traverse the mountain road followed by Ladmirault's infantry, the 2nd Division prepared to attack the commanding position held by the Austrian 5th Corps.

The 1st Division (Forey) had left Esenta about 4 a.m., passed through Castighone, and followed the road by Le Grole, while Bazaine, with the 3rd Division, marched in rear of Forey,

When on the afternoon of the 23rd the 5th Austrian Corps had occupied Solferino with outposts on the hills to the west, the picquets furnished by Bils' brigade reported the. presence of large bodies of the enemy in their front, and Stadion was satisfied that a general action must take place on the morrow, and he therefore fortified his positions as far as possible.

These picquets at once noted and reported the French advance against Medole early on the 24th, as also the movements of the 1st French Corps against Stadion's position; but the Austrian outposts were none the less driven in by the French, and fell back upon the battalions occupying Le Grole and the hills in the vicinity. Le Grole was in turn captured after some very sharp fighting, and the defenders then retired upon their reserves, holding the next line of hills some 3,000 yards in front of Solferino.

The battle for the possession of these heights was protracted and bloody, but they were taken about 10 o'clock, and the French were then able to move forward and place upon them several guns which engaged the Austrian pieces about Solferino. Stadion had long since informed Count Schlick of the attack which was pressing upon him, and the 1st and 7th Corps were moved up close in support, while Mensdorff's cavalry left Bregnedolo and moved into the open country between the Casa Morino and Cassiano.

On the left of the French centre Ladmirault was gaining but little ground, and even that with great sacrifice, but Baraguey now found himself able to send forward his remaining division—that of Bazaine—as the Emperor Napoleon, who had now himself reached this part of the field, had deployed the two infantry divisions of the Guard in support. Already Bils' brigade, which had suffered grievously, had begun to give ground, and the brigades of Festetics and Puchner had fallen back to the heights round the village of Solferino and had occupied the houses, the cemetery and the Monte di Cipressi.

Here they had been reinforced by several battalions from the brigades of Hoditz and Paszthory of the 1st Corps, which had reached the scene of action. The troops were all well covered behind walls and inside the houses and offered for long a formidable resistance, but the French were at last able, after great difficulties and with immense loss, to bring a battery on to the heights, and at a range of 300 yards to open fire upon the cemetery and attempt to batter down its walls.

The Italian Army had passed the night of the 23rd in the following positions: the 2nd Division (Fanti) at Malocco maintained touch with Baraguey d'Hilliers; the 1st (Durando) and 5th (Cucchiari) were in bivouac about Lonato; the 3rd (Mollard) was at Rivoltella, while the 4th (Galdini) had been sent north towards Tyrol in support of Garibaldi. The 1st, 3rd, and 5th Divisions were each ordered to send forward on the 24th strong reconnoitring columns towards Pozzolengo, and in accordance with these instructions Durando dispatched at 4 a.m. a brigade, which, on reaching Venzago about 5.30, detached two battalions, two guns and two squadrons towards Pozzolengo. These found Madonna della Scoperta occupied by the enemy and their advanced troops became engaged.

Cucchiari in like manner had sent forward a similar detachment, which left Lonato at 3 a.m., passed through Desenzano, followed the railway for some distance and then turned south towards Pozzolengo.

Mollard sent out no fewer than four such reconnoitring parties, and all came more or less in contact with the Austrians in position in front of Pozzolengo and Madonna della Scoperta; but this breaking up of the Italian forces into numerous small and independent columns, effectually prevented King Victor Emmanuel from disposing usefully of masses of troops, and exercised a baneful influence upon the action of his army as a whole, from which it suffered throughout the remainder of the day.

The 8th Corps had bivouacked on the night of the 23rd with all its brigades in and around Pozzolengo, whence it was to have marched next day in three columns upon Lonato and Desenzano. About 6.30 a.m., however, the advance of the Italians upon Pozzolengo was detected and Benedek at once placed four brigades on the hills covering the town from the west, holding back in reserve the greater part of two complete brigades. These arrangements were more than sufficient; the various Italian columns attacked the positions held by the Austrians, but were easily driven back upon the brigades in rear.

The Austrians then pursuing, possessed themselves of the high ground about San Martino, but not being at the moment sufficiently strongly supported, found it necessary to fall back. Benedek had by now realised that he had no longer to deal with mere reconnoitring parties, but that practically the whole Italian Army was in his front, and deciding, if possible, to seize the strong position of San Martino, he attacked it with three brigades, and after heavy fighting succeeded in there establishing himself.

He was not, however, to be permitted to remain there undisturbed; between 9 and 10 o'clock Cucchiari's division advanced from the direction of Rivoltella, and being joined by one of Mollard's brigades, threw itself against the Austrians. The attack, at first successful, was repulsed with loss and Cucchiari's troops fell back across the railway to Rivoltella and San Zeno to reform.

By 10.30, then, all the Italian attempts in this portion of the field had been heavily defeated, and for something like two hours there was no resumption of hostilities in this quarter. Benedek, however, did not dare to pursue; the 5th Corps on his left was still heavily engaged, and it seemed best to the commander of the 8th Corps not to uncover his left flank by any premature advance.

Meanwhile the 2nd Piedmontese Division (Fanti) was at last in movement from the vicinity of Malocco, where it had long been awaiting orders. The Emperor Napoleon had sent for the division to support Baraguey's attack upon Solferino, but while on the march to the centre Victor Emmanuel, seeing the turn which events had taken in the northern part of the field, directed Fanti to move to the help of the Italians, ordering him to place one brigade under the orders of Mollard, while Fanti himself proceeded with the other towards Madonna della Scoperta to assist Durando.

The Emperor Napoleon had now established himself in front of the centre near the heights which Baraguey's troops had captured, and he was convinced that here lay the key of the whole of the Austrian position. Neither on the right or left had any real impression as yet been made upon the enemy's battle line, and the Emperor now decided to attempt to help the efforts of his flanks by breaking through in the centre. He then ordered d'Alton's brigade of Forey's division (which had not yet been engaged) to advance, but it was received with so terrible a fire that it was unable to push far forward, and General Forey, who had himself led the brigade, then called for reinforcements. These were at once forthcoming: Camou's division of the Imperial Guard was ordered to support Baraguey's corps—Picard's brigade being directed along the heights to the left, while that of Manèque supported d'Alton.

This fresh attack was irresistible; covered by the fire of two batteries of the artillery of the Guard, the Tower and the Monte di Cipressi were now taken with a rush, while further to the left Bazaine—whose batteries had been pounding the walls of the cemetery—now sent forward his infantry. Joined by some battalions of Ladmirault's division the cemetery was now stormed and finally carried with the bayonet, and the defenders, falling back, evacuated the village of Solferino, leaving several guns and many prisoners in the hands of the French.

While these events were passing in the centre, MacMahon—hearing from Niel that he was about to move on Cavriana—was now able to take ground to his left and connect with the Guard. He therefore gave instructions to La Motterouge to march on Solferino, followed by the 2nd Division under Decaen. To obviate the danger of any gap being thus formed between his own corps and Desvaux's Cavalry Division, MacMahon ordered the cavalry of the Guard—which had been placed at his disposal—to take post on his right. In the south General Niel, who with his single corps had more than stood his ground against the troops of Schwartzenberg and Schaffgotsche, now, about 11 a.m., saw the heads of the columns of another Austrian corps—that of Weigl—entering upon the field from the direction of Castel Grimaldo.

Vinoy had by this time turned Crenneville's men out of the

farm north of Baite, but to capture and hold it, as also the line Rebecca—Baite—main road, against all the attacks of the Austrians, had used up practically the whole of Niel's reserves. At last, however, his repeated calls upon Canrobert for co-operation met with some response; Renault's division of the 3rd Corps had already been sent to cover de Luzy's right flank south of Rebecca, and becoming easier in his mind in regard to the approach of the mythical men from Mantua, Canrobert placed one of Trochu's brigades at Niel's disposal, retaining the other at Medole, while Bourbaki's division remained near Castel Goffredo to watch the roads from the south and southeast.

In the centre Ladmirault, whose division had suffered heavily, was left to hold Solferino; Bazaine was directed to follow Stadion, who had retired towards Pozzolengo; Forey's division, with the Guard, was ordered on Cavriana; while MacMahon moved forward upon Cassiano—which was occupied without much difficulty—and then stormed the Monte Fontana in rear, held by two brigades of the 7th Corps. This, too, was captured and guns brought up to it. It was now about 2 p.m. MacMahon, then, seeing that the Guard had not yet been able to get up into line with him, and that the Austrians were now again threatening to strike between himself and Niel, decided to make no onward movement for the present and to content himself with merely holding his ground. The Austrians, however, made a desperate attempt to regain possession of the hill, and for some time their adversaries had considerable difficulty in retaining possession, and it was not indeed until MacMahon had ordered a general advance of his whole corps, supported by a powerful artillery and a brigade of the Imperial Guard, that the remnant of the two gallant Austrian brigades of Wallon and Wussin were finally swept off the Monte Fontana and hurled back to Cavriana, where shells were already falling.

Supported now by the fire of forty-two guns, Niel in the south was still holding out against his numerous foes, and strengthened by the arrival of the brigade brought him by Trochu, and which he placed in rear of his centre, he even threw forward the few troops he still had in hand to the attack of Guidizzolo. This village was, however, held in great strength and the battalions which Niel had sent against it were obliged to fall back upon Baite. Canrobert had now at last, about 3 p.m., satisfied himself that the right of the army was in no danger of surprise, and he therefore drew Bourbaki's division from the neighbourhood of Castel Goffredo nearer to the 4th Corps, whereupon Niel ordered Trochu to send Bataille's brigade to the attack of Guidizzolo.

The Commander of the First Austrian Army had, ere this, received orders from his Emperor to endeavour to relieve the pressure on the centre by bringing round his left and then striking with his whole strength at the flank of the French centre. It was, however, already impossible to carry out the Emperor's wishes. The 3rd and 9th Corps could not now be withdrawn from the actions in their front and set free to seek a fresh objective in a new direction; the cavalry had left the field; and the 11th Corps—which as a body might yet have been used effectively—had been drained away in driblets to fill up gaps and to strengthen weak points.

The few infantry reserves, too, which now emerged from Guidizzolo, preparatory to marching on Cassiano and Solferino, were charged and checked by the French cavalry of the Guard connecting MacMahon and Niel.

Bataille's brigade moved with great *élan* upon Guidizzolo, but although the Austrians were driven in and many prisoners were taken, the French were unable to penetrate into the town.

In the centre, however, the Guard and the 2nd Corps had now captured Cavriana, and in the northern part of the field only had the Austrians been able to hold—and more than hold—their own.

The four brigades in Benedek's front line had endured and beaten back the attacks of the Italian divisions of Mollard and Cucchiari, and had indeed so completely overthrown them that about 1 o'clock the battle in this portion of the field had died down, and for some two hours there was no more heard "the voice of them that shout for mastery and the noise of them that cry, being overcome." Benedek was still in ignorance of the fact that Cialdini's division was detached and that Durando was engaged about Madonna della Scoperta with the right wing of the 5th Corps. He only knew with whom he had been fighting, and had no idea by whom the action might be renewed.

After two o'clock, as the Italians were again gathering for the attack, Benedek heard of the renewal of the assault, in overwhelming force, upon Solferino, and received an order from Count Schlick to endeavour to make a diversion against the left of the French. This was shortly followed by a query from Imperial Headquarters whether it was possible for the 8th Corps to detach troops to the assistance of the Austrians about Solferino. Benedek wisely decided that neither of these proposals were practicable and that he could best help to gain the day by the defeat of the enemy already in his front.

It was clear to him that the King of Italy had not yet fully developed his attack and the force in his front seemed to be momentarily increasing in strength. To send any real help to Solferino he must detach at least two complete brigades, and he did not feel any confidence that he could at the most hold his ground with the troops then remaining, while the loss of his position would entail that of Pozzolengo, in rear of which lay the line of retreat of the Second Army.

About 3 p.m., the first reports reaching Benedek of the commencement of the retreat of the 5th Corps, he withdrew four battalions from his position and sent General Reichlin with them to occupy some hills to the south and south-west of Pozzolengo, so as both to secure the right flank of the 8th Corps and also cover the retirement of the 5th, Reichlin reached his intended position about 4 p.m.—relieving there the rearguard of the 5th Corps—and was almost immediately attacked by the brigade Piedmont of Fanti's division, which, ordered to support Durando, had pushed forward by Madonna della Scoperta, then vacated by the troops under Stadion. Since then Mollard, with Fanti's other brigade, was at this moment preparing to attack

San Martino in front, while Cucchiari was operating against it from the direction of Rivoltella and San Zeno, it will be realized that Benedek's position was thus endangered from three sides.

Shortly after four o'clock the 8th Corps received orders to retire and cross the Mincio at Salionze. Benedek, however, was determined to hold his ground until the 5th Corps had got well away and until he had sent off his wounded and trains; it seemed clear to him, too, that any attempt to cross at Salionze with his whole corps must interfere with Stadion's retirement, so he arranged for two brigades with the ammunition reserve columns to pass the river at Peschiera.

About 5 o'clock a tremendous rain and thunderstorm—accompanied by intense darkness—broke over the whole field, and in other portions of it put an end to the fighting and assisted the Austrian retreat; in front of San Martino, however, the battle was resumed and continued to rage.

Reichlin was driven from his position and forced to retire on Monzarabano, but the remainder of the corps fought magnificently up to and during the retreat, which Benedek only commenced about 9 p.m.—himself leading one last desperate counter-attack which overthrew the Italians and secured a practically unmolested retirement for the much-tried 8th Corps. By 3 a.m. on the 25th the passage of the Mincio was accomplished, as arranged, at Sahonze and Peschiera.

The First Army had fallen back long before. As early as 2 p.m. Wimpffen, having no cavalry at hand, seeing no signs of the 2nd Corps, and all his reserves having long since been thrown into the fight, had reported to the Emperor Franz Josef that he could no longer hold his ground; he directed that the 9th Corps should fall back upon Goito, the 3rd by Cerlungo to Ferri, while the 11th Corps covered the retreat of both and eventually retired by Goito to Roverbella. When about 3 p.m. the Emperor heard of the capture of Solferino and Cassiano and the retreat of the 5th and 1st Corps, he gave instructions that the 5th Corps should fall back fighting to Pozzolengo, and that Schlick—gathering up all the still effective units of the Second Army—should take up a fresh position about Cavriana and hold his ground there as long as possible.

The Austrian Emperor did not at that time regard the loss of Solferino as implying the loss of the battle, and hoped that with the 1st and 7th Corps he might yet be able to hold back the French in the centre, while the stroke which he had ordered Wimpffen to make fell upon the flank of the advancing enemy. But it was not long before news reached the Emperor at Cavriana that the First Army had already begun to fall back and therewith vanished all hope of re-establishing the fight. The Emperor then ordered a retreat behind the Mincio, and Schlick—directing the 7th to make as protracted a stand as possible at Cavriana and at Volta—withdrew his remaining corps from the battlefield.

The fatigue of the Allies, and the heavy storm which at 5 p.m. descended upon the field, put an end to the fighting and checked all pursuit; the Austrian corps fell back unhindered, and by the evening of the 25th they had all regained the positions on the left bank of the Mincio which they had quitted on the morning of the 23rd. Even then, however, the rest they so greatly needed was not assured, for the Emperor Franz Josef directed that in the event of any serious attack upon the line of the Mincio on the 25th, the retreat should be continued to the banks of the Adige.

The losses sustained by the units of both armies were as follows:—

AUSTRIANS.

First Army:—	Officers	men
3rd Corps	109	3,098
9th ,, ...	130	4,219
11th ,, ...	61	2,140
Zedtwitz's Cavalry Div.	2	37
Second Army:—		
1st Corps	90	2,734
5th ,, ...	124	4,318
7th ,, ...	34	1,844

8th ,, ...	79	2,536
Mensdorff's Cavalry Div	10	172

Grand Total	639 officers and 21,098 men
Of which there were killed	94 officers 2,198 men
,, ,, ,, wounded 500	10,307
,, ,, ,, missing 45	8,593

ALLIES.

	Killed	Wounded	Missing
Imperial Guard	181	704	63
1st Corps .	610	3,162	659
2nd ,, ..	234	986	275
3rd ,, ..	37	257	19
4th ,, . ,.	560	3,421	502.
Italian Army	691	3,572	1,268
Grand Total	2,313	12,102	2,776

Out of which the French had 117 officers killed and 644 wounded; the Italians had 49 officers killed and 167 wounded. The casualties among the senior officers was very heavy on both sides; the Austrians had four general officers wounded, the French five and the Italians two, and of these latter two of the French and one of the Italians died of their wounds. Among, too, those of junior rank, who this day died for France, there was one who bore a name associated with the triumphs of the First Napoleon upon Italian soil; this was Lieutenant-Colonel Junot, Duke of Abrantes, Chief of the Staff to General de Failly.

That night the Allied Army bivouacked where the end of the battle had left them—the troops of Victor Emmanuel at San Martino, the 1st French Corps at Solferino, the 2nd at Cavriana, the 3rd at Rebecco, the 4th between Medole and Guidizzolo, the Guard and Imperial Headquarters at Cavriana, and the cavalry of Desvaux and Fartouueaux about Guidizzolo.

Of the battle itself Hamley says:

"There was no exhibition on either side of strategical art; none of the movements on either side since the battle of Magenta had altered the chances of success; and the result was altogether due to tactics."

He cites the battle of Solferino as a good illustration of the necessity for moving as compactly and as nearly in fighting order as possible when in the vicinity of the enemy.

"Both armies," he says, "had reconnoitred the country between Chiese and Mincio; each expected to find its adversaries awaiting it behind the river; neither anticipated the encounter; but the French Army was by far the best prepared for it by the order of its march."

Further Hamley points out that the peculiar conformation of the hill of Solferino—the back steep, scarped and accessible by but one winding path and with nearly two miles of broken ground between it and the hills about Cavriana—minimised its advantage as an advanced post in front of the general position; he would have had it either left altogether unoccupied or have advanced the whole line of battle so as to include it.

The cause of the victory of the Allies at Solferino, Moltke finds in the better leading of the French, but above all in the fact that the Austrian Commander had no general reserve anywhere at his own disposal. The Austrian Army, too, had only quite recently been reorganised, and the three years' term of universal military service had been only some two years established, so that the army was practically composed of recruits. The supply arrangements of the Austrians were throughout faulty and frequently came altogether to a standstill. The actual rations were insufficient for men enduring the the hardships of field service, since they only received half a pound of meat a man *per diem* and were not permiitted to cook their food oftener than once in twenty-four hours.

To the objection made by some that the Austrians fought with a river at their backs, Lecomte points out that in this particular case, where the Mincio was spanned by numerous bridges and also covered by two fortresses, the usual dangers and inconveniences of such a position were reduced to a minimum. The best proof of the correctness of his assertion is that the Austrian retirement was easily and rapidly conducted, although at the same time it is not improbable that a knowledge of the risks of their position induced them to fall back full early.

Rüstow seeks the chief reasons for the Austrian overthrow in the fact that owing to the Austrian force having been divided into two armies, the Emperor Franz Josef—nominally the commander-in-chief—had no troops, and especially no general reserve, at his own disposal, and that consequently each army fought for its own hand.

Further, up to and after 10 a.m. the Austrian Staff refused to believe that a general action had long since commenced, and thrust brigade after brigade, as each came up, into the fight, where they were at once overpowered by superior numbers at the particular point, so that when any real reinforcement was required none was to hand. But Rüstow very truly remarks that it was not gun or rifle or even tactics which won the day at Solferino, but the offensive spirit which was wanting in the Austrian leaders; and in support of this statement he points out that the Austrians, who crossed the Mincio simply and solely to attack the Allies, had no sooner met them than they took up defensive positions.

Chapter 10

The Peace of Villafranca

After the battle of Solferino—whereat the French claim to have captured two Colours, thirty guns and 6,000 prisoners—no pursuit of the Austrians was attempted, even on the 25th, on which day the French moved quietly forward—the 1st Corps to the vicinity of Pozzolengo and the 4th to Volta. The rest of the Allied Army remained in the positions of the previous night with the exception that the 3rd Corps replaced the 1st at Solferino, leaving one of its divisions at Guidizzolo with the cavalry of Desvaux and Partouneaux.

The Austrians, on recrossing the Mincio, had either destroyed or prepared for destruction all the bridges in their rear; orders had been issued, as has been already mentioned, that in the event of serious attack the Mincio line was not to be held, but that the army should fall back behind the Adige; on the morning of the 27th, however, a fresh order was given out that the troops should hold their ground, making none the less every preparation for orderly retirement in case of need. In the course of the day the Emperor Franz Josef visited the Headquarters of both armies, and, in reply to inquiries, was assured by their commanders that it was doubtful whether their men would stand against any real attack and the advisability of retirement behind the Adige was urged.

The Emperor then finally decided that the army should withdraw from the line of the Mincio, and that night the outposts of both armies fell quietly back; leaving the bivouac fires alight, the

Austrians retired, and during the course of the 28th the Second Army was already in position on the left bank of the Adige and about Verona, the First Army falling into line the next day.

The Emperor Napoleon had decided that, prior to marching on Verona, it was necessary to reduce the fortress of Peschiera, the possession of which was important to cover his main line of operations, to serve as a base for any onward movements, and to assure, if such became necessary, his line of retreat. The siege operations had been entrusted to the Italians, who took up a line from Ponti to Rivoltella, and on the 26th Baraguey d'Hilliers pushed one of his divisions on to Monzambano in their support. On the 28th the 1st Corps crossed the river to Casa Prentina, while on the day following, Niel—who for his share in the victory of Solferino had been created a marshal of France—moved to Borghetto and Valeggio, the Italians establishing on the 30th their 5th Division at Salionze.

On July 1 the Headquarters of King Victor Emmanuel were moved to Pozzolengo, his 3rd and 5th Divisions were placed on the left of the 1st Corps, and the investment of Peschiera was complete. On this day the whole of the remainder of the French Army was transferred to the left bank of the Mincio, crossing at Monzambano, Borghetto and Pozzolo, and occupied positions—the 1st Corps at Oliosi, the 2nd at Santa Lucia, and the 4th at Oustoza; the whole of the rest of the French Army was about Valeggio, except Bourbaki's division, which was at Goito. The cavalry were occupied in pushing forward parties towards Mantua, and also towards the Oglio to meet Prince Napoleon, whose corps actually joined the main army on the 3rd.

On the 2nd MacMahon had moved to Villafranca and Niel to Sommacompagna, while the 1st Corps occupied Castelnuovo and Cavalcaselle.

The measured movements of the Allies, which had given the enemy breathing time after the battle of Solferino, are said to have been due, in the first instance, to a deficiency of supplies and to the fact that these, even when forthcoming, could not be brought up, as all transport was required for the evacuation of the wounded of both armies—one might almost say of all three, since very many of the Austrian wounded had of necessity been left on the field; in the second instance, to the tardy arrival of the material required for the prosecution of the siege of Peschiera. Already on June 16 orders had been sent to France to expedite the dispatch of the necessary siege guns, for which the projectiles and the fuses were still in course of manufacture in French arsenals. On July 3, however, part of the siege park arrived at Pozzolengo, and a week later the French were able to commence the establishment of their batteries before Peschiera.

A very brief account must now be given of the operations which had been carried out in the mountains of Tyrol and of those which were projected on the sea. We have seen that the 6th Corps shared with the main army in the alternate advances and retirements dictated by the vacillating methods of the Austrian Headquarter Staff, and that its commander had been ordered to support the westward movement of June 23, which culminated in the defeat at Solferino, by pushing forward towards Salo and Gavardo. At this time Austrian garrisons were besieged in Rocca d'Anfo and Bagolina; the latter place fell and the required advance to Salo was now scarcely practicable and was not indeed carried out, the 6th Corps falling back to cover the approaches to the Upper Adige.

On the 26th, Cialdini's division had occupied Aprica, Edolo, Breno, Lavenone and Salo, while Garibaldi's troops had advanced into the Valtelin; the principal valleys and the westward approaches thereto, being thus held and safeguarded, there was no longer any fear for the left flank and rear of the Allied Army, since the 6th Corps was thus held completely in check. The troops under Cialdini and Garibaldi—the latter was early in July at Tirano with eleven battalions and several independent companies—were not to be the only force available for service in the mountains. Another infantry division, that of General Hugues, left France on July 3, and was sent on to Brescia, there to form a support to the Italian troops operating in Tyrol.

The navy, too, was ready to effect a diversion by striking

at Venice, which had been blockaded since June 1 by a small squadron under Rear-Admiral Jurien de la Gravière. On June 12 the main fleet sailed from Toulon and arrived on the 21st at Antivari, where, being joined by four Italian ships, Admiral Romain Desfosses now united under his command 50 ships of war, mounting 800 guns. From Antivari the fleet proceeded to the Island of Lossini, which had been chosen to serve as an advanced base for future naval operations; the island is only a few hours' sail from Venice and is almost equi-distant from Trieste, Pola, Fiume and Zara.

The orders given to the Admiral in command were to force an entrance to the harbour of Venice, penetrate into the lagoons and bombard the forts. The ships had only embarked 1,000 infantry and artillery for landing purposes, but it was the intention of the Emperor Napoleon to send forward, at a favourable moment, a corps to operate from Venice upon the Austrian communications. General Wimpffen—who had been promoted from brigadier after Magenta—was nominated to the command of the military forces intended to be landed upon the shores of the Adriatic, and a body of 8,000 men had been ordered to embark in Algeria to form the nucleus of such a force.

There are three main channels of approach to Venice—that by the Lido, by Malamocco and by Chioggia, and the last had been selected as the point where the fleet should force an entrance.

The following then were the dispositions of the Emperor Napoleon for carrying on the war: on the left, by the operations of Cialdini and Garibaldi, to threaten the Austrian right and the line of the Adige; in the centre, having possessed himself of Peschiera, to capture Verona; and with the fleet to attack and seize Venice, using that town as a base whence to launch attacks upon the Austrian line of communications.

But at this moment the Emperor Napoleon discovered signs that the prosecution of the war might possibly result in its being no longer confined to the three Powers now engaged, and that France might be called upon to fight not only on the Adige but also on the Rhine. He decided then that it would be inexpedient to risk "*ce qu'il n'est permis à un souverain de mettre en jeu que pour l'indépendance de son pays*," and being desirous of discovering the views of the Emperor of Austria, he sent General Fleury to him at Verona on July 6, proposing a suspension of arms.

At the same time he wisely made all preparations for the continuation of the siege of Peschiera and for the protection of the besieging force; and with this object the French Army took up a position next morning on the hills bordering the Tione, having its left at Castelnuovo, where was the 1st Corps, its right at Valeggio held by the 3rd, the centre being made up by the 4th Corps at Oliosi and the 2nd at Santa Lucia; in rear were the 5th Corps and the Imperial Guard.

In the meantime, however. General Fleury had returned from Verona with the acceptance of the proposed armistice, and all hostile movements both by land and sea were at once suspended. The terms of the armistice signed on the 8th, provided for a suspension of arms until August 15, and for lines of demarcation between the respective armies; but on the 11th there was a meeting between the two emperors at Villafranca, and the conditions of peace—finally ratified at Zürich in the following November—were then discussed and afterwards drawn up. By this treaty Austria was to cede Lombardy to Napoleon, who was then to hand it over to Piedmont; the Italian States were to be amalgamated into a confederation under the Pope; but Venice, though forming part of this confederation, was to remain under Austrian rule.

Napoleon had entered upon the campaign announcing his intention of "freeing Italy from the Alps to the Adriatic." It has been said, however, "that he wished Italy to be free, but did not want Italian unity; rather did he desire the formation of a confederacy wherein France could always make her own predominance felt in the Peninsula." Circumstances in the end, however, proved to be too strong for him; the provisional government in Florence suddenly determined to unite Tuscany to Piedmont, and Romagna, Emilia, Parma and Modena at once followed suit. "In the convention of Plombières it had been agreed that in the event of a kingdom of eleven million inhabitants being established from the Alps to the Adriatic, Piedmont would cede Savoy to France. As, however, by the treaty of Villafranca, Venetia had remained under the Austrian yoke, no more had been said about cession of territory, but, by the annexation of Central Italy, the number of Victor Emmanuel's subjects was now augmented to eleven million. In order to induce Napoleon to approve of such an annexation, Cavour offered him Savoy, but the Emperor claimed Nice as well." These were ceded to France in March, 1860, and thus, by a strange irony of fate. Savoy, the cradle of the dynasty whose reigning representative had made Italy a king- dom, and Nice Garibaldi's native province, became the spoils of the Ally.

LEONAUR

ALSO FROM LEONAUR
AVAILABLE IN SOFTCOVER OR HARDCOVER WITH DUST JACKET

CAPTAIN OF THE 95th (Rifles) *by Jonathan Leach*—An officer of Wellington's Sharpshooters during the Peninsular, South of France and Waterloo Campaigns of the Napoleonic Wars.

BUGLER AND OFFICER OF THE RIFLES *by William Green & Harry Smith* With the 95th (Rifles) during the Peninsular & Waterloo Campaigns of the Napoleonic Wars

BAYONETS, BUGLES AND BONNETS *by James 'Thomas' Todd*—Experiences of hard soldiering with the 71st Foot - the Highland Light Infantry - through many battles of the Napoleonic wars including the Peninsular & Waterloo Campaigns

THE ADVENTURES OF A LIGHT DRAGOON *by George Farmer & G.R. Gleig*—A cavalryman during the Peninsular & Waterloo Campaigns, in captivity & at the siege of Bhurtpore, India

THE COMPLEAT RIFLEMAN HARRIS *by Benjamin Harris as told to & transcribed by Captain Henry Curling*—The adventures of a soldier of the 95th (Rifles) during the Peninsular Campaign of the Napoleonic Wars

WITH WELLINGTON'S LIGHT CAVALRY *by William Tomkinson*—The Experiences of an officer of the 16th Light Dragoons in the Peninsular and Waterloo campaigns of the Napoleonic Wars.

SURTEES OF THE RIFLES *by William Surtees*—A Soldier of the 95th (Rifles) in the Peninsular campaign of the Napoleonic Wars.

ENSIGN BELL IN THE PENINSULAR WAR *by George Bell*—The Experiences of a young British Soldier of the 34th Regiment 'The Cumberland Gentlemen' in the Napoleonic wars.

WITH THE LIGHT DIVISION by *John H. Cooke*—The Experiences of an Officer of the 43rd Light Infantry in the Peninsula and South of France During the Napoleonic Wars

NAPOLEON'S IMPERIAL GUARD: FROM MARENGO TO WATERLOO by *J. T. Headley*—This is the story of Napoleon's Imperial Guard from the bearskin caps of the grenadiers to the flamboyance of their mounted chasseurs, their principal characters and the men who commanded them.

BATTLES & SIEGES OF THE PENINSULAR WAR by *W. H. Fitchett*—Corunna, Busaco, Albuera, Ciudad Rodrigo, Badajos, Salamanca, San Sebastian & Others

LEONAUR

ALSO FROM LEONAUR
AVAILABLE IN SOFTCOVER OR HARDCOVER WITH DUST JACKET

WELLINGTON AND THE PYRENEES CAMPAIGN VOLUME I: FROM VITORIA TO THE BIDASSOA *by F. C. Beatson*—The final phase of the campaign in the Iberian Peninsula.

WELLINGTON AND THE INVASION OF FRANCE VOLUME II: THE BIDASSOA TO THE BATTLE OF THE NIVELLE *by F. C. Beatson*—The second of Beatson's series on the fall of Revolutionary France published by Leonaur, the reader is once again taken into the centre of Wellington's strategic and tactical genius.

WELLINGTON AND THE FALL OF FRANCE VOLUME III: THE GAVES AND THE BATTLE OF ORTHEZ *by F. C. Beatson*—This final chapter of F. C. Beatson's brilliant trilogy shows the 'captain of the age' at his most inspired and makes all three books essential additions to any Peninsular War library.

NAVAL BATTLES OF THE NAPOLEONIC WARS *by W. H. Fitchett*—Cape St. Vincent, the Nile, Cadiz, Copenhagen, Trafalgar & Others

SERGEANT GUILLEMARD: THE MAN WHO SHOT NELSON? *by Robert Guillemard*—A Soldier of the Infantry of the French Army of Napoleon on Campaign Throughout Europe

WITH THE GUARDS ACROSS THE PYRENEES *by Robert Batty*—The Experiences of a British Officer of Wellington's Army During the Battles for the Fall of Napoleonic France, 1813.

A STAFF OFFICER IN THE PENINSULA *by E. W. Buckham*—An Officer of the British Staff Corps Cavalry During the Peninsula Campaign of the Napoleonic Wars

THE LEIPZIG CAMPAIGN: 1813—NAPOLEON AND THE "BATTLE OF THE NATIONS" *by F. N. Maude*—Colonel Maude's analysis of Napoleon's campaign of 1813.

BUGEAUD: A PACK WITH A BATON *by Thomas Robert Bugeaud*—The Early Campaigns of a Soldier of Napoleon's Army Who Would Become a Marshal of France.

TWO LEONAUR ORIGINALS

SERGEANT NICOL *by Daniel Nicol*—The Experiences of a Gordon Highlander During the Napoleonic Wars in Egypt, the Peninsula and France.

WATERLOO RECOLLECTIONS *by Frederick Llewellyn*—Rare First Hand Accounts, Letters, Reports and Retellings from the Campaign of 1815.

CPSIA information can be obtained at www.ICGtesting.com
Printed in the USA
270609BV00001B/141/P

9 781846 777134